Did He Say That?

Did He Say That?

The Difficult Words of Jesus

Charles Sigel

Mitchell Mackinem

WIPF & STOCK · Eugene, Oregon

Wipf & Stock
An Imprint of Wipf and Stock Publishers
199 W. 8th Ave., Suite 3
Eugene, OR 97401

www.wipfandstock.com

PAPERBACK ISBN: 978-1-4982-8061-7
HARDCOVER ISBN: 978-1-4982-8063-1
EBOOK ISBN: 978-1-4982-8062-4

Manufactured in the U.S.A.

The authors wish to dedicate this work to God, who, in Jesus, "loved us and freed us from our sins by his own blood."
—Rev 1:5

"Neither height nor depth, nor anything else in all creation, will be able to separate us from the love of God that is in Christ Jesus our Lord."
—Rom 8:39

Contents

Acknowledgments

Dr. Mackinem gratefully acknowledges the contributions of Earlene Hinkle, who read the first drafts and provided helpful insights along the way. The Reverend Dr. Wayne Kannaday provided a thoughtful review and suggestions early in the process. Deepest thanks to Beth for her unending support. Finally, thanks to his friend Charlie, who is the best of scholars.

Dr. Sigel acknowledges his indebtedness to Dr. Mitchell Mackinem, who for more than a year has been urging him to undertake this project. Not only that, Dr. Mackinem recorded it and edited the material (a thankless task) and sought out a publisher. Had it not been for his encouragement and active participation, this work would never have seen the light of day. On the other hand, since Dr. Sigel was the original preparer and presenter of the material, he insists all errors and shortcomings must be laid at his doorstep.

Introduction

THIS BOOK WAS DEVELOPED from a series of lectures given by Dr. Sigel in a Sunday school class. In writing this book, we sought to use the same tone and activities we rely upon in our Sunday school classes in the hope that Sunday school teachers everywhere will be able to use this book to launch their own highly successful classes. However, this book's early readers found it to be a valuable personal study course as well. Based on our early readers' encouragement, we rewrote the book with the aim of making *Did He Say That?* as useful at a kitchen table as it is in the classroom. Of course, it takes a little imagination and adaptability to read a Sunday school book as a personal study course, but as authors, we hope we have made it just as easy for you to complete the activities by yourself as it will be to lead a classroom of people through this book's many helpful activities and valuable lessons.

1

How to Read the Bible

THERE ARE MANY DIFFERENT ways to read the Bible. Some people will read a passage in English and then just take that passage in whatever way it strikes them. People have successfully the read the Bible this way for many years.

Others are what we call "cherry pickers." They will look at a passage (for example, one about giving money) and track down every line in the entire Bible that refers to that passage. Then they will pull these many passages together to create some sort of unified picture.

Historians read the Bible as a historical narrative documenting the life and times of people who lived in a specific place. Classical scholars might see the Bible as shining a small light on the ancient world. In fact, there are as many approaches to reading the Bible as there are people.

Basic Assumptions

For us, the Bible is the inspired word of God in matters of faith and life. By "inspired" we mean the traditional idea that God breathed his life-giving breath into the word. From this beginning, we start with several basic assumptions about what we think the Bible is and how we might approach it.

First, the Bible is a long document written by many people over thousands of years. It is a story of the relationship between

God and humans. We believe it is the story of how God has reached out to humankind over the millennia. We do not believe it to be a historical narrative, although history is in the narrative. We do not believe it to be a book of wisdom, although wisdom is certainly found there. It is not a blueprint for government, although there is much to be learned about governing. We do not believe it is a business document, although business leaders would do well to pay attention. It is a book of faithful people engaged in their ongoing quest to be in relationship with God and to understand God in their own lives.

Second, each book in the Bible reflects the person(s) who composed it, the time it was written, the audience for whom it was intended, and, most importantly, the understanding of God at that time and in that place. The earliest of the gospels, according to many scholars, is the Gospel of Mark, which was written around sixty years after the birth of Christ. The last of the four gospels is John's, which was written at least one hundred years after the birth of Christ. Between the writing of the Gospel of Mark and the writing of the Gospel of John, the Romans had destroyed the temple, the Romans had killed Jews by the tens of thousands, the Gentiles had moved into Israel, and John's world in general had become very different from the world of Mark. Their respective Gospels reflect these differences.

Third, the Bible was not composed in English. The Bible was written in Hebrew, Aramaic, and Greek. People have since translated these ancient languages into English. As with any translation, there are difficulties. Some Greek words do not translate well. Some English words carry connotations that would not have been there in the Greek. If many Aramaic and Greek words simply do not translate over into English, then there will be many legitimate versions based on different translations of the Bible. Remember, a committee produced the King James Bible, and the same is true for most popular Bible translations and versions.

Fourth, there is no one definitive, original Bible. There are no "original" books or letters. For every book of the Bible, there are hundreds and often thousands of ancient copies of the text. These copies were made by hand by scribes and do not fully agree with each other. It is often the case that 80 percent of the manuscript is consistent with all other known versions, 10 percent is close to other translations, and the remainder add or subtract words and phrases that do not match the other manuscripts. For the majority of these competing texts, any discrepancies tend to be quite small. For example, verb tenses and spelling are among the most common differences. Occasionally we find significant differences, however, making it difficult for scholars to try to piece together what the original document said.

Taken as a whole, the Bible is a living document full of humanity. It is not a fully transcribed, easily translated, and understandable book. The Bible warrants careful and thoughtful exploration and examination.

How to Read the Bible: The Basics

We suggest a simple approach to reading the Bible. There are five steps to reading any specific biblical passage. A passage need not be a single line but can instead be a collection of sentences that form a specific whole. In Greek, we call this a *logion*. As we go through this book together, you will see that we use the same basic approach:

1. What does the passage say?

2. How does that passage fit within its textual context?

3. What would the people of that day have heard?

4. What does this passage tell us about God?

5. What does this passage say to us, today?

After a brief explanation of these steps, we will look at a specific passage to see how each step might be applied.

In order to understand what a passage says, it is important for us to understand the many different ways its words can be translated and used. Remember that words not only have denotations, which are precise meanings or definitions, but also connotations, which are the word's associated meanings. If we look at the word "law," we find many denotations and connotations. Law is usually some type of code proscribing what cannot be done. Criminal and civil law holds a different meaning for us than Old Testament law, while hearing a pastor described as "too much on the law" evokes still another understanding. The point is that without modifying words for context, the word "law" tells us little. The Greek words often used in the New Testament pose the same problem as the word "law." Unfortunately, very few of us read ancient Greek, so we cannot simply go and read the documents for ourselves. Instead, we have to rely on different translations to figure out the exact meaning of the words of Scripture. Luckily, we have some readily available tools to help us examine the meanings of words. Without the ability to read biblical Greek, an Amplified Bible or study Bible can help us to identify and come to understand interesting words and phrases.

No specific passage exists independently from the text immediately before and after it. Larger passages surrounding a particular line are critically important to understanding how that line was meant to be interpreted. Much of Sunday school is spent trying to parse out these exact meanings based on context. Often we can develop a fuller understanding by placing a short passage within the proper textual context. With context, we can begin to ask, how would people at the time this particular passage was composed have heard it? Here, the danger we run into is anachronisms. Anachronisms occur when modern-day interpreters project an idea or understanding from the present onto the past. For example, if we were to dress the magi like the wizard Gandalf from *The Lord of the Rings*, we would be taking a late twentieth-century interpretation of a fantasy wise man and placing it upon a first-century nomadic teacher. This habit, of course, leads to errors. Another example is our picture of hell. Most of the modern understandings of hell come from Dante's *Inferno* and not biblical passages. Putting a red-tailed devil in the desert with Jesus during the forty days is a mistake.

It is difficult to understand the mind of God. God reveals the divine self through word, deed, and the sacraments. If we can understand what a passage says (its biblical context and how the people of first-century Israel saw the passage) we can then begin to contemplate how that passage affects our own understanding of God. Some passages offer a clear reference to God, and we can simply point to that passage as telling us something about God. It is not so easy when Jesus tells us a parable. As authors, we suggest that when Jesus speaks, he speaks for God as a prophet. Furthermore, when Jesus speaks, he not only speaks as a prophet, but also as someone in a unique relationship with God. In this way, when Jesus talks we can hear the voice of God. Based on what he says, we can understand more about God's nature and his ongoing relationship with us.

Finally, only after we have carefully examined all the preceding questions can we then ask the question of what a passage says to us as Christians in the twenty-first century. We do not start with "What does this passage mean to me?" Rather, we conclude with "What does this passage say to us?" Here, we take the voice of God and look at the world around us, ourselves, our community, and our church as we ask ourselves, "What is God saying to us?" The danger we have seen is that God often seems to agree with an individual's perspective. If you find that God often agrees with you, maybe this is not about the voice of God but rather about your need to seek justification for what you believe. We believe the voice of God often challenges, threatens, confounds, and provokes us as Christians in and of the world, and so God's voice is best heard and understood within a Christian community setting. Understanding the word of God is a communal process.

Application of the Method

An extended example is probably one of the best ways to understand how to apply this method. For example, let us start with a fairly simple and straightforward passage, Luke 15:1–2 (NIV).

DID HE SAY THAT?

The Parable of the Lost Sheep

Now the tax collectors and sinners were all gathering around to hear Jesus. But the Pharisees and the teachers of the law muttered, "This man welcomes sinners and eats with them."

—LUKE 15:1–2

At first, this looks like a simple passage. But let us apply our method and see what we learn. First, we note that the title "The Parable of the Lost Sheep" is not part of the biblical text. This is an aid added much later to help people quickly navigate their Bibles.

For our purposes, we will use the New International Version's text. A good first step in examining what the passage actually says is to look at several other translations of Luke 15:1–2:

> "Then drew near unto him all the publicans and sinners for to hear him. And the Pharisees and scribes murmured, saying, 'This man receiveth sinners, and eateth with them'" (KJV).

> "Now all the tax collectors and sinners were coming near to listen to him. And the Pharisees and the scribes were grumbling and saying, 'This fellow welcomes sinners and eats with them'" (NRSV).

> "Jesus became increasingly popular among notorious sinners—tax collectors and other social outcasts. The Pharisees and religious scholars noticed this. Pharisees and Religious Scholars: 'This man welcomes immoral people and enjoys their company over a meal!'" (The Voice).

How different these translations are! The King James Version was written during the Elizabethan period in England (1611). This was not the first English translation of the Bible, and it replaced the earlier Geneva Version (1568). Over fifty scholars worked for over two years to develop this "Bible to end all Bibles." Yet today's English language is very different from of English of the 1600s. Even with this in mind, we can see the difference between the words "murmur" and "grumbling" used in the New Revised Standard Version compared to the "muttering" we see used in the New International Version. Finally, we have The Voice, which is a very modern interpretation of the biblical passages and describes the religious scholars "noticing."

Pay attention to what is not said. The Pharisees do not "confront" Jesus. The religious scholars do not "challenge" Jesus. Muttering, grumbling, and murmuring all suggest that there was a low tone of complaint not meant for Jesus's ears.

One of our favorite tricks is to use an Amplified Bible. An Amplified Bible inserts all the different meanings of a word (both definitions and connotations) in any given passage. Look at the passage in the Amplified version: "Now the tax collectors and [notorious and (a) especially wicked] sinners were all coming near to [Jesus] to listen to Him. And the Pharisees and the scribes kept muttering and indignantly complaining, saying, 'This man accepts and receives and welcomes [(b) preeminently wicked] sinners and eats with them'" (Amplified Bible).

Notice that different words appear in brackets and within those brackets are parenthetical references to footnotes that indicate where these translations come from. For this passage, those alternative words come from Joseph Thayer's *A Greek-English Lexicon*. For those of us who do not read Greek, these amplifications can be quite helpful.

In looking at the Amplified translation, it becomes clear that in every version of this passage the sinners in question are not just average sinners. In every translation, the sinners appear to be notorious, wicked, and outside the bounds of normal sin. Not only was Jesus talking to notorious sinners, he was also eating a meal with them. For Jews in the ancient world, eating a meal together was a sign of social acceptance, recognition, and a certain amount of hospitality. Jesus was not lecturing the sinners on sin. He ate with them as if they were his friends. This certainly would have challenged the ideas of religious leaders at the time.

These two passages need to be placed within a larger context. The larger context is the two parables that Jesus offers following the first two verses. The first parable is that of the man who searches for his lost sheep. The second is the parable of the woman who searches for her small coin. Both of these parables offer great comfort to those who are sinful and unclean. Both speak to the people who are likely to have been thrown away by the religious establishment.

> Now the tax collectors and sinners were all gathering around to hear Jesus. But the Pharisees and the teachers of the law muttered, "This man welcomes sinners and eats with them." Then Jesus told them this parable: Suppose one of you has a hundred sheep and loses one of them. Doesn't he leave the ninety-nine in the open country and go after the lost sheep until he finds it? And when he finds it, he joyfully puts it on his shoulders and goes home. Then he calls his friends and neighbors together and says, "Rejoice with me; I have found my lost sheep." I tell you that in the same way there will be more rejoicing in heaven over one sinner who repents than over ninety-nine righteous persons who do not need to repent. Or suppose a woman has ten silver coins and loses one. Doesn't she light a lamp, sweep the house and search carefully until she finds it? And when she finds it, she calls her friends and neighbors together and says, "Rejoice with me; I have found my lost coin." In the same way, I tell you, there is rejoicing in the presence of the angels of God over one sinner who repents. (Luke 15:1–10)

We note that the word "repent" has many meanings. For modern people, repentance might mean to turn away from sin and sin no more. The Greek word for repentance is *metanoia*, which can alternatively be understood as a change of mind for the better, heartily amending one's ways, or abhorrence of one's past sins. When Jesus speaks of repentance at the end of the verse 10, he is calling for people to amend their ways or change their mind. It certainly does not mean to be sinless from that day forward.

Commentaries are a good way to gain insight into a passage. Several commentators note that this opening of Luke 15 is the amazing scene where the bad people are listening seriously and deeply to Jesus and the people that are supposed to be their religious leaders are off to the side, grumbling and complaining. These religious leaders could have listened to Jesus—they could have engaged the teacher—but instead they withdrew and complained. Notorious sinners and tax collectors and the worst of people took the words of Christ seriously and sat attentively. The irony of this is inescapable. Those who should have understood Jesus misunderstood him, and those who should have had no idea about Jesus understood him. This insight just touches the surface of what commentaries can bring to bear on a given passage.

What does this tell us about God? Here we have to speculate about what we understand the nature of God to be. For example, if you see God as wrathful, the passage might be a warning to clean up your act so as to be worthy of God's effort to find you. The focus shifts from the searcher to the searched. If you believe, as we do, that God is a God of grace and forgiveness, then the passages speak to us as sinners. Jesus was clearly addressing the worst of sinners in this passage. Jesus did not cite the law to them, chapter and verse, although he was certainly capable of doing so. Instead of condemning them, Jesus offered a parable in which the lost is the most valuable of commodities. We believe that what this passage tells us, then, is that a God of grace and forgiveness seeks us. We have a God who wants desperately to be in communion with us. God will seek us out in the wild places and in the dark corners.

What does this passage say to us as twenty-first-century Christians? In looking at this passage, the first aspect that struck us is whom we identify with. As we read these two simple lines, do we identify with the religious leaders grumbling over whether Jesus was paying them enough attention or spending too much time with those terrible people? Or do we identify with the most notorious of sinners? We suggest that we identify not with the religious leaders (although many of us may in fact be religious leaders) but with the most notorious of sinners. If we see ourselves as the worst sinners, who are we to criticize others? We suggest that the passage tells us of a God who rejoices at bringing the lost back into the fold. We believe this passage is a comfort to sinners and warning against religious leaders. As the old song says, "I was once lost but now am found."

Your Turn

To practice further, try to apply this method to Mark: 40–41:

> A man with leprosy came to him and begged him on his knees, "If you are willing, you can make me clean." Jesus was indignant. He reached out his hand and touched the man. "I am willing," he said. "Be clean!" Immediately the leprosy left him and he was cleansed.

Here are a few questions to help you on your way:

1. How was leprosy understood in the ancient world?
2. How would those in Jesus's day understand touching a leper?
3. Is the word "indignant" the only possible translation of the word at the end of the first sentence in verse 41?

The word "immediately" is interesting. Is it a common word for Mark or for the other gospel writers?

1. What was the rest of the story after this passage?
2. What happened before this passage?
3. What does Jesus's willingness to touch a leper tell us about God?
4. Who or what are the lepers of today?

2

Eunuchs?

Opening Prayer

Precious God, we thank you for your word, for its truth, for its power, and for its promises and challenges. We thank you that we can gather around the word and feel the presence of your Holy Spirit. Guide, direct, and open our hearts and minds. We pray for all this to your Son, Jesus Christ, our Lord. Amen.

Opening

What does Jesus ask us to do?

Teacher suggestion: Make a short list.

Here are a few ideas we came up with. Speak up if you disagree.

- Jesus asks that we love our enemies.
- Jesus asks that we pray for those who oppose us.
- Jesus asks that we sell what we have.
- Jesus asks us to leave our families.
- Jesus asks us, speaking directly to males now, to castrate ourselves.

To be blunt, a eunuch is a man who has been castrated. In Latin, they are called *castratus*. Eunuchs were common in the ancient world. The word "eunuch" may come from the Greek for "bed-guard," *eunen echein*. The "bed guard" brings to mind the idea of eunuchs as the guards of harems. Eunuchs were popular during the time of the Roman Republic. After the end of the Republic, during the Roman Empire, eunuchs increased in popularity. They ranged from pretty-boy, slave catamites (young boys who were sexual slaves) to court officials. Eunuchs appealed to both men and women because they were thought to be impotent. For Roman matrons, this was a definite advantage. Since eunuchs were often familiar with the intimate areas of the Imperial court, they became associated with political power and intrigue.

Eunuchs were also a common feature in eastern mystic religions. Priests serving the Phrygian goddess Cybele (called Magna Mater by the Romans) would castrate themselves as a sign of their devotion. The Cult of Magna Mater, or of the Great Mother, was a very old and widely popular religion during the Roman Republic and early Imperial Rome.

In modern times, some male members of the Heaven's Gate apocalyptic cult were castrated in order to lead a more ascetic lifestyle. The cult members committed mass suicide in March of 1997. They believed suicide was the only way to reach what they believed was an alien spacecraft following the Hale-Bopp comet.

The Word

The disciples said to him, "If this is the situation between a husband and wife, it is better not to marry." Jesus replied, "Not everyone can accept this word, but only those to whom it has been given. For there are eunuchs who were born that way, and there are eunuchs who have been made eunuchs by others—and there are those who choose to live like eunuchs for the sake of the kingdom of heaven. The one who can accept this should accept it."

—MATT 19:10–12

What an odd little passage. Did Jesus really just say that it is good that some men castrate themselves for the kingdom of heaven? What in the world could this possibly mean? It sounds as if Jesus is saying this practice is good because it's for the goodness of the kingdom.

Take a few minutes to brainstorm some ideas.

This verse requires careful examination. Let us take it one step at a time. This passage presents three problems:

1. This verse about castration occurs only in Matthew.

2. This text is a radical text.

3. This text seems to conflict with what we know about Jesus's character.

೮ාCଓ

Eusebius Pamphilus on Origen: "At this time while Origen was conducting catechetical instruction at Alexandria, a deed was done by him which evidenced an immature and youthful mind, but at the same time gave the highest proof of faith and continence. For he took the words, 'There are eunuchs who have made themselves eunuchs for the kingdom of heaven's sake,'" in too literal and extreme a sense. And in order to fulfill the Saviour's word, and at the same time to take away from the unbelievers all opportunity for scandal,— for, although young, he met for the study of divine things with women as well as men,—he carried out in action the word of the Saviour.

೮ා Cଓ

The first big decision we must make is: Was Jesus being literal or figurative in his expression? One person who thought the passage was literal was Origen (185–254 CE) a great third-century church father who took this passage literally. Origen was so in tune with God's will that he castrated himself for the sake of the kingdom. I think generally people would say he went too far.

Was Jesus speaking literally, given his knowledge of these kinds of religious groups? Why or why not?

If you take Jesus's words figuratively, you are probably right, because Matthew sets the passage in the context of divorce and remarriage. If the passage were literal, it would not have been in that context.

If this passage is figurative, let us explore what it could mean apart from any context. Are there any other places where Jesus might have said something about self-mutilation?

See if anyone can recall or look up a relevant passage.

The passage that likely comes to mind is Mark 9:42–50:

> If anyone causes one of these little ones—those who believe in me—to stumble, it would be better for them if a large millstone were hung around their neck and they were thrown into the sea. If your hand causes you to stumble, cut it off. It is better for you to enter life maimed than with two hands to go into hell, where the fire never goes out. And if your foot causes you to stumble, cut it off. It is better for you to enter life crippled than to have two feet and be thrown into hell. And if your eye causes you to stumble, pluck it out. It is better for you to enter the kingdom of God with one eye than to have two eyes and be thrown into hell, where "the worms that eat them do not die, and the fire is not quenched." Everyone will be salted with fire. Salt is good, but if it loses its saltiness, how can you make it salty again? Have salt among yourselves, and be at peace with each other.

The question we have for this text from Mark is the same as the one we asked of the passage from Matthew: Is Mark speaking figuratively or literally? In the Markan text, we see this setting to be a figurative one. Before this passage, the disciples come to Jesus and raise questions about an individual who is performing miracles but not following Jesus. Jesus says, "No, do not stop him. Let him go. Anyone not against me is for me" (Mark 9:40). Then Jesus moves on to the question of the little ones.

If anyone causes one of these "little ones" to sin (here the Greek word is *skandalizo*), it is better for that person to have a millstone tied around his neck and be thrown into the depths of the sea. Immediately thereafter, Jesus begins to talk about sinning: "if your hand causes you to sin" and so forth. The issue here is that of discipleship. As bad as it is for anyone to cause the "little ones" to sin so, it is worse for the disciples to mislead the little ones. Some translations use the phrase "cause to stumble," which is part of the Greek word *skandalizo*. You could say that this is the context for the passage from Mark. If we lift those words about "cutting off your hand" out of that context, then what are we left with?

At that juncture, we must look to the Jesus tradition for an answer. Nowhere in all of the Jesus traditions do we see any hands mutilated for religious reasons. In fact, when Jesus faces the woman in the throes of adultery he does not say, "Circumcise her." He says, "Forgive her." When Peter denies Jesus three times, Jesus forgives him. Jesus does not say he "will cut out your tongue." Nowhere in any of the Jesus traditions do we see Jesus suggesting mutilation. Therefore, we do not see in the Markan text or the Jesus tradition any indication that these words should be taken literally. Of course, Jesus then immediately uses the word "salt," and clearly that is a metaphor. Taken together, these considerations clearly point to the fact that Jesus did not intend to say literally, "Cut off their hands." Rather, he was talking about the responsibilities of discipleship.

If the Matt 19 passage is figurative, there are three potential figurative meanings. Let us look at each one in turn.

Jesus could be figuratively saying, "Never get married." He might urge that we do not get married for the sake of the kingdom. This would be a figurative way of castrating oneself. Celibacy is for a lifetime, or it is at least a long-term lifestyle. The term "celibacy" implies never getting married because of this lifetime commitment. What is the difference between celibacy and abstinence? Abstinence implies a certain temporariness, not necessarily a complete lifestyle change. Could abstinence mean not having sex as a marital couple for the sake of the kingdom? How difficult would that be in a modern marriage?

There certainly are examples of platonic marriages. People can live together in a harmonious relationship with no conjugal contact. For example, at the height of the Victorian period, some couples eschewed sex or greatly limited it, since sex was thought to dirty or sully the woman.

Second, could Jesus have figuratively meant, "If you are married, give up sexual pleasure?"

A third alternative is that one should not remarry after divorce. This could be stretching the word "eunuch" fairly far.

Think about sex and ice cream. If you have never had ice cream, you don't know what you're missing. One of the authors of this book is lactose intolerant, so he has not eaten ice cream in over thirty years. He still misses it. Is sexual intimacy like that? Once you have had it, does it become difficult to go without? We suspect so, because once a couple has been together in an intimate relationship, both partners know what they are missing.

In chapter 15 of Leviticus, we find a passage about seven verses long in which males are specifically told to not drop their seeds on the ground. While it may make us uncomfortable, we need to discuss these things. What could this mean? It seems reasonable to think that the passage means males should not masturbate.

Leviticus contains many passages that people find objectionable. Despite this discomfort, these passages are part of the Bible and Torah. In Matt 15:16, Jesus was speaking to a Jewish group. Jesus is saying that for the observant Jew, once you get married and divorced, you do not get married again. Thus a Jew who had experienced sexual pleasure would now be deprived of ice cream, so to speak. Maybe this reading is not so far-fetched. There are three basic possibilities: celibacy, abstinence, or no remarriage after divorce.

The Context

With those possibilities in mind, we need to ask another question: What type of setting did Matthew insert this passage into? What is the context in which this individual passage appears?

> When Jesus had finished saying these things, he left Galilee and went into the region of Judea to the other side of the Jordan. Large crowds followed him, and he healed them there. Some Pharisees came to him to test him. They asked, "Is it lawful for a man to divorce his wife for any and every reason?" "Haven't you read," he replied, "that at the beginning the Creator 'made them male and female,' and said, 'For this reason a man will leave his father and mother and be united to his wife, and the two will become one flesh'? So they are no longer two, but one flesh. Therefore what God has joined together, let no one separate." "Why then," they asked, "did Moses command that a man give his wife a certificate of divorce and send her away?" Jesus replied, "Moses permitted you to divorce your wives because your hearts were hard. But it was not this way from the beginning. I tell you that anyone who divorces his wife, except for sexual immorality, and marries another woman commits adultery." The disciples said to him, "If this is the situation between a husband and wife, it is better not to marry." Jesus replied, "Not everyone can accept this word, but only those to whom it has been given. For there are eunuchs who were born that way, and there are eunuchs who have been made eunuchs by others—and there are those who choose to live like eunuchs for the sake of the kingdom of heaven. The one who can accept this should accept it."

After reading this longer passage, how can we understand the context of Jesus's words? Divorce? A quick, surface reading seems clear: if you get divorced, do not remarry. Of the three possible interpretations, which of the three fits the passage best? What figurative possibilities best fit Matthew's context?

Take a vote in class. Maybe participants can explain which
position they favor and why.

Fundamental to the context of Matthew is the idea that you do not remarry after divorce. Let us see if we can follow the movement of the argument. Jesus said if you get divorced, there is no remarriage. Then the disciples ask, "Is it better not to get married at all?" The disciples might be thinking it is too hard to go from a sexual life to an asexual life. Jesus responds, "Well, not everyone can bear this, only those who are so constituted." Then in verse 12 Jesus says, "for," which means "because." Verse 12 becomes an explanation of verse 11. Not everyone can bear this, because there are only a few who castrate themselves for the kingdom.

If we assume that Matthew is talking figuratively, then he is talking about no remarriage after divorce. Of course, Matthew's passage does allow for divorce in cases of infidelity.

The problem with the surface reading is the passage about Moses. Go back and look at it if you missed it. Jesus is a Jew. He does not say that Moses got it wrong. Jesus comments that Moses allowed divorce because of the "hardness of your heart."

Jesus has essentially separated the world of today and "hardness of heart" from the way God intended. In separating the beginning from now, Jesus points out what God's intention was. When we live in an age of hard hearts, Moses may be right. Divorce is allowed because of our hardness of heart, not God's will. Divorce is not what God intended in the beginning. Now we live in a different age. We live in another age of heard hearts. Jesus was aware of that, and we are aware. Therefore, maybe Moses was right. There can be remarriage after divorce. However, in the beginning it was not so.

The material about divorce is in several of the gospels and gospel sources. The divorce passage occurs both in Mark and Q source material. For Mark, the reference is found in chapter 9. In the Q tradition, we find are passages about both marriage and divorce. Luke 16:18 is an example of that: "Anyone who divorces his wife and marries another woman commits adultery, and the man who marries a divorced woman commits adultery." Only in Matthew do we see that business of castrates. Back to figurative eunuchs.

What did Jesus mean with this particular passage?
List some possibilities

Some scholars have speculated that probably the castration text was not originally attached to the divorce passages. Since Mark, as the earliest version, does not have the castrate text but does have the divorce passage, the castrate passage was likely added later.

It seems reasonable, given the other gospels, that the castrate passage circulated independently from the divorce passage. Let us take it out of the context of the divorce passage and asked what this particular passage meant for Jesus.

There are two possibilities.

First, it may have been directed by Jesus's opponents to John the Baptist and Jesus. Jesus and John the Baptist were referred to as castrates because neither was married. The first chapter of Genesis clearly points out that people should be fruitful and multiply. The Torah specifically encourages people to get married, which neither Jesus nor John the Baptist did.

Since neither Jesus nor John was married, they were operating against Jewish tradition and law, both of which encouraged people to marry and have children. Therefore, one way this text can be interpreted is that Jesus's opponents intended the word "castrate" as a slander.

There is a second possibility: this passage did not target Jesus but rather his twelve disciples. If the opponents aimed these insults at Jesus's twelve disciples, what were the disciples doing to earn this slander? It may be because the Twelve had abandoned their wives. Jesus said to all his disciples, "Come and follow me," and they left their families. Maybe critics aimed the term at the disciples in a pejorative way. Since the disciples had turned their backs on their marital responsibilities, "the eunuch" might metaphorically apply to them. Paul's letters indicate that Peter was definitely married:

> Am I not free? Am I not an apostle? Have I not seen Jesus
> our Lord? Are you not the result of my work in the Lord?
> Even though I may not be an apostle to others, surely I
> am to you! For you are the seal of my apostleship in the

Lord. This is my defense to those who sit in judgment on me. Don't we have the right to food and drink? Don't we have the right to take a believing wife along with us, as do the other apostles and the Lord's brothers and Cephas? Or is it only I and Barnabas who lack the right to not work for a living? (1 Cor 9:1–6)

Clearly, some of the apostles had wives that accompanied them, as did Jesus's brothers.

What Does It Mean for Us?

We live in a modern world where castration is rare and unusual. We could all too easily cast off this passage as some vestige of ancient times. Our modern culture has little place for castration. Certainly, we live in a culture that values sex and family. Sexual behavior and sexuality are common features of popular culture. It is hard to watch a movie or television where there is not either a veiled or explicit reference to sexual behavior. We also live in a society that places high priority upon family and family life. Many couples will go to extraordinary lengths to conceive or adopt children. After looking at this passage, its historical context, and its context within Matthew, we are left with the question "What does this passage say about us?"

To examine the possible applications of this passage, let us look at the Roman Catholic position. The Roman Catholic interpretation of this text becomes very important in the context of the Roman Catholic Church. Let us consider two Latin words: *ordinarii* and *perfecti*.

Roman Catholic theology makes a distinction between *ordinarius* and *perfectus*. Most of us are the ordinary Christians; the *ordinarii*. The *perfectus* is a different class; they are the Christians who belong to the religious orders, including sisters, brothers, priests, and so forth.

The Roman Catholic Church goes further. The responsibility to God for *ordinarii* is to keep the Ten Commandments. They are to live by the Ten Commandments.

For the religious, or *perfecti*, there are the evangelical councils or the councils for perfection. The three councils for perfection are charity, obedience, and chastity. The councils for perfection are not required to receive eternal life; rather, they are enhancements for those wishing to live a holy life or to perform so-called "acts of supererogation."

The Roman Catholic Church turns to this passage to justify chastity. This justifies an absolute life of celibacy. However, the text of Matt 19:10–12 does not necessarily say that. The Roman Catholic Church reads it as an institutional command: "This you must do!" Protestants do not read it as a command.

As you may know, many Roman Catholic brothers and sisters wear a wedding band because of their marriage to Christ. When they are married to Christ, their relationship is better than that of ordinary Christians. The Roman Catholic Church lays it down as an institutional command for life, although the passage does not say that.

The Roman Catholic viewpoint is not congruent with mainstream America. For Protestants, family life is a high priority, so it is difficult for us to understand how this text about castration applies to us.

I am going to make a suggestion. First, let us look at two guiding ideas. First, the individual must show a willingness to forego family life. Despite the overwhelming challenge, some people are willing to figuratively castrate themselves for the sake of the kingdom.

Second, consider the voluntary nature of the figurative castration. The text indicates that this castration is a gift and not an imposition. Jesus does not command men to be castrated, reject sex, or never marry after divorce. Some people can do this as a willing sacrifice, but it is not required.

Let us consider two examples. Frankie San, a noteworthy pastor in South Carolina, dedicated his life to working with prisoners at the oldest and toughest state prison. Now demolished, the Central Correctional Institute was built before the Civil War and housed many dangerous, discarded, and disgraced men. Reverend

San spent his entire professional life as pastor to the prisoners for the sake of the kingdom. He never considered marriage or children because his "children" were the prisoners he ministered to.

The second example is the case of a seminarian who happened to be homosexual. He had a long-term relationship, but when this seminarian went into the ministry, he gave up romantic involvement with his partner. He has since lived his whole life as a seminarian separated from his partner, except for occasional visits. He sacrificed that part of his relationship for the sake of the congregation.

Closing

We wonder whether the texts speak more directly to these examples than the Roman Catholic interpretation does. It does not speak to us as family people. The Roman Catholic interpretation does remind us, however, that there are some Christians who do extraordinary things. These acts of sacrifice might even challenge our basic beliefs about family life.

Discussion Questions

In what ways does the call to discipleship fit with a family life, and in what ways does it not fit? Does sacrificing for the sake of the kingdom make you a "better" Christian than those who do not sacrifice in the same way? In what ways do we separate some people into the *perfecti* and not others? The Christian church has a long and difficult history with sexuality, ranging from the belief that all sex is sinful to the idea that only certain types of sex are acceptable. What is your understanding of your church's views on sexuality?

3

Camels and Needles

Opening Prayer

GRACIOUS GOD, WE THANK you that with all the turmoil of life with all of its confusion, you are nevertheless our God. In that knowledge, we look to you for guidance, Father. We look to you for guidance and forgiveness and for help in those places where we are afraid to enter. Through us, in us, and with us, your name may be glorified. In Jesus's name, amen.

Opening

Be warned that you may leave today's session more confused than when we started. There may even be more confusion than enlightenment.

As a little exercise, let us start by listing the large animals that existed in Jesus's time in Palestine.

Here are ten clues that might help you. Watch out for terrible puns.

1. David reportedly slew this one. (lion)

2. _____ feathers. (horse)

3. Dr. _____ and Mr. Hyde. (jackal)

4. A greeting, "Hi, Lena!" (hyena)

5. Leo X's invective against Luther:
   "a wild _____ has invaded." (boar)

6. _____ donuts. (donkey)

7. The Pooh _____. (bear)

8. A Geico commercial, "hump day." (camel)

9. Hiding one's head in the sand. (ostrich)

10. Jesus compared himself with this one, "Take my yoke." (ox)

These are ten of the largest animals in Palestine during Jesus's day. Of all the animals we just listed, which one would the people of Palestine have considered the largest? Obviously, it is the camel. There are two obvious things about the camel: First, it is quite large. Second, the camel is ungainly; it is not a graceful animal. When Jesus said it is easier for a camel to pass through the eye of a needle than for a rich person to enter the kingdom of God, you can see why he uses that specific animal. The camel is the largest of animals, and the eye of the needle is the smallest of openings. The camel is the most ungainly of animals, and the needle is the sleekest of household items.

The Word

Again I tell you, it is easier for a camel to go through the eye of a needle than for someone who is rich to enter the kingdom of God.

—MATT 19:24

Let us start by looking at the camel and the eye of the needle. Can this be Jesus? I am not asking whether these words truly belong to Jesus or not—that is another point. Rather, could Jesus have used a saying that is at once so silly and yet so hard? Aside from the silliness of the mental picture it draws, if taken at face value, this passage suggests that no one with any wealth may enter heaven. To eliminate an entire group of people seems contrary to a message of repentance and salvation, which is hard indeed. Early scholars tried to wiggle out of the silliness and hardness. Bible scholars of an earlier generation simply believed this passage was too preposterous for Jesus to have used. Why would someone as devout and reverent as Jesus use such a ridiculous analogy? If he was not ridiculous, could Jesus have been so hard? To sidestep the silliness and hardness, scholars tried different approaches.

Read this phrase aloud and listen to the words:
"A pair of pairs."

There are several different ways to spell out this phrase and still be correct. For example, "a pair of pears."

These are homonyms. They have the same sound but are spelled differently. The word in Greek for camel is *kamelos*. Some scholars have spelled it *kamilos*. This word means "rope." Some scholars have suggested that Jesus meant rope, not a camel. Jesus would then be saying, "It is harder for a rich person to enter the kingdom God than to put a rope through the eye of a needle." Of course, no matter how intriguing this possible translation error is, there is absolutely no evidence that this is the case. No Greek manuscripts of Matthew show the word *kamilos* instead of *kamelos*. Lacking evidence, we are still stuck with the camel and the needle. Again, everybody knows you cannot get a camel through the eye of the needle, so why did Jesus say such a ridiculous thing?

ဒာ၈

Archeology has proven an interesting tool in examining biblical passages. An important archeological site is Sepphoris. This was a large town located about one hour's walk north of Nazareth. Herod Antipas chose this site in 4 B.C. as the capital of his government. During the time Jesus was in his 20s, carpenters and other workers built and expanded the town. It is intriguing to think that Jesus might have worked in such a large, urban, and diverse town. Maybe Jesus's tolerance of Gentiles came from his years working in Sepphoris.

ဒာ၈

A second approach to the passage proposes that there was a small gate in the walls of Jerusalem called the "eye of the needle." Once Jerusalem's main gate was closed in the evening, anyone entering or leaving the city would have had to go through this small gate. A camel attempting to enter or exit would have had to prostrate itself and crawl through this narrow gate. For a number of years, the gate theory showed up in commentaries. The problem is that there is no archaeological evidence that any "eye of the needle" gate existed.

If we eliminate the rope theory and the gate theory, we are back to a camel passing through the eye of a needle. If Jesus intended those words to be taken seriously, why would he use such a preposterous image?

The Context

Let us look at the entire passage found in Matt 19:16–26:

> Just then a man came up to Jesus and asked, "Teacher, what good thing must I do to get eternal life?" "Why do you ask me about what is good?" Jesus replied. "There is only One who is good. If you want to enter life, keep the commandments." "Which ones?" he inquired. Jesus replied, "'You shall not murder, you shall not commit adultery, you shall not steal, you shall not give false testimony, honor your father and mother,' and 'love your neighbor as yourself.'" "All these I have kept," the young man said. "What do I still lack?" Jesus answered, "If you want to be perfect, go, sell your possessions, and give to the poor, and you will have treasure in heaven. Then come, follow me." When the young man heard this, he went away sad, because he had great wealth. Then Jesus said to his disciples, "Truly I tell you, it is hard for someone who is rich to enter the kingdom of heaven. Again I tell you, it is easier for a camel to go through the eye of a needle than for someone who is rich to enter the kingdom of God." When the disciples heard this, they were greatly astonished and asked, "Who then can be saved?" Jesus

looked at them and said, "With man this is impossible,
but with God all things are possible".

Similar passages occur in Mark and Luke. It may be fanciful, but
we can imagine the interchange between the rich man and Jesus
like a police drama. Recalling an old television show, let us talk
about *Columbo*. Peter Faulk played Columbo. The detective ap-
peared disheveled, disorganized, and somewhat forgetful. His
appearance was a ruse that made other people overestimate their
cleverness, and in this way, Columbo was often able to catch the
murderer. We can imagine Jesus standing with a rich man and acting somewhat like Columbo. Jesus goes through all the commandments and turns to walk away. Just as the rich man jumps in and
proclaims loudly that he has kept all the commandments, Jesus
turns around, having laid a little trap, and adds one more thing. Of
course, that "one more thing" is quite large, and it knocks the rich
man out of discipleship.

Looking at the entire passage, there are several reasons for
why Jesus may have used this preposterous example. First, notice
that when Jesus utters the saying about the camel and the eye of a
needle, the disciples respond, "Well, then who can be saved?" The
disciples are shocked. One way to understand the passage is that
Jesus intended to shock the people, particularly the disciples, by
using this preposterous example.

Second, it is possible that Jesus intended to pronounce that
it is absolutely impossible for a rich man to enter the kingdom. It
is just as impossible as it would be for a camel to crawl through
the eye of a sewing needle. There is no softening the passage; he
offered a stark message: Rich people cannot enter the kingdom of
heaven.

Third, Jesus may have intended to use humor. *All in the Family*
was a groundbreaking television show. The show broached many
controversial subjects, most notably race relations. If the show had
been a drama, it might not have been as effective as it was as a
comedy. Comedy has a way of sneaking in a serious message under the cover of good fun. In laughing, we are not only laughing
at ourselves, we are also coming to understand something about

ourselves. *All in the Family*'s Archie Bunker character was famous for his insensitive and even racist remarks. You and I know that a lot of the people who laughed at Archie Bunker in fact began to recognize that they said some of the same things as Archie. In review, there are three possible reasons for Jesus to have said such a hard and silly thing: for shock value, to underscore impossibility, or for humor.

The entire passage still leaves us with a number of questions. To explore the passage further, let us look at a number of statements about what Jesus might have meant. Ask yourself, "What does this text say to us?" as you think about each of the following statements.

Have people vote on whether they agree or disagree with each of the following statements. Remember, if you agree, then you need to "walk the walk."

- Sell everything you own.
- Get rid of everything that gives you personal security.
- Keep only what is needed for life's necessities.
- Just follow Jesus, forgetting everything else.
- The passage applies only to rich people, not to me.
- The passage is meant for only the few, the "religious" few.
- Jesus is speaking spiritually, not literally.
- Jesus's words are exaggerated, and so they must be nuanced to fit the "real" world.

If you do not like any of these passages, what do you think Jesus is actually saying?

Collect all of the responses and put them on the board.

What Does It Mean for Us?

For us, this passage is particularly difficult. As we have seen, scholars have tried to avoid the silliness and hardness of the passage. Some pastoral approaches might provide a way out. Author Mitchell Mackinem has a friend who is very religious. This friend's life has run the gambit religiously. Right now, he observes the Roman Catholic tradition, although he's dissatisfied with it. He started in the Southern Baptist Church. He taught at a religious college. He was part of the Presbyterian Church for a while. He has also been deeply involved in Eastern religions like Buddhism. He has been to seminary. Before his retirement, he was a clinical psychologist, and he has always been a deeply intellectual man. He once came to Mitchell very upset by this text because he interpreted it as saying, "Sell everything you've got." This friend had given away lots of money to charitable causes, and even in retirement, he asked himself, "What more can I give?" When he came forward, disturbed about this passage, Mitchell treated this text pastorally.

Mitchell pointed out that Jesus did not ask all his disciples to sell everything. His friend thought that was an interesting point, and it inspired a new insight: not every Christian must sell everything either. Maybe this passage was directed specifically to the rich man because something else was getting in the way, meaning it was not simply a question of riches. As a pastor, Mitchell could offer the idea that the passage is not about the man's finances but rather the man's heart. If the rich man is focused on "I" and "me," then he cannot be focused on "us" and "them." Maybe Jesus is not calling for us to sell things but rather to focus on the needs of others. These pastoral answers offer convenient ways to wiggle out from this difficult passage. Many of us want to ameliorate the hardness of this text. The pastoral answers do avoid the preposterous and hardness of the passage. This is the danger.

Another way to wiggle out from underneath this text is to point out that the text is talking about the rich, and so it does not apply to those who are not rich. When asked, most people think people who make a little more money than they do are wealthy.

Most people honestly see themselves as "just getting by" and not wealthy. "Rich" need not mean that one has more than ten million dollars, ten thousand dollars, or even one dollar. We can all easily argue that since we are not rich by whatever standards we create, we need not worry about this passage.

A third way to interpret this question is that it was not the man's wealth that was the problem but rather that the man was not keeping the first commandment. The first commandment says, "I am the Lord your God, who brought you out of the land of Egypt, you shall have no other gods before me" (Exod 20:2–3). Perhaps Jesus saw that riches were the man's god. Jesus was challenging the man's devotion, his adoration, his allegiance, and his loyalty. Riches might be something getting in the way of his allegiance to God. Let us keep our rigid interpretation of the text, without any rationale or excuses. Let us ask this question: "Is Jesus being too hard on wealth?"

Have the class take a vote.

As a follow-up question, let us ask, "What can wealth do?"

List all the positive things wealth can do.

Here is a list that we came up with:

- Money can provide jobs for other people.
- Money can keep us healthy.
- Money opens up opportunities for us.
- We can give money to charity.
- Money allows us to preserve the things we care about.
- Money allows for expanded choices.
- Money provides opportunities for investment.
- We can use money to create foundations or fund public works.

So far, we have focused on how money can help other people. In addition, money can do a lot for the people who have it. Research shows that people with higher incomes are less likely to experience health problems, less likely to suffer mental health problems, less likely to divorce, less likely to be victims of crime, live longer, have fewer marital arguments, and have children who experience more academic success.[1] Of course, not everyone agrees that money is necessarily good for either the person it belongs to or for everyone else.

Some of the opportunities money provides are bad things. Money can be spent on illicit drugs, prostitution, strip clubs, extravagance, and excess. If Jesus is being appropriately hard on those with money, it is fair to ask what kinds of bad things money can do.

Try coming up with your own list of
bad things money can lead to.

Here are some things we came up with:

- Indulgence
- Excess
- Extravagance
- Self-centeredness
- Self-gratification
- Illusionary security

After looking at both lists, ask yourself the following question: "What does this passage mean to me?" There are three clues in the biblical passage we can look at.

Reread the entire passage and see if
you can identify any clues.

The first clue is that Jesus tells the rich man to sell his things and give to the poor. Riches tend to drive a wedge between the haves and have-nots. Jesus might be telling this man to build bridges rather than walls that separate us. Jesus may be telling us

1 See "Education and Socioeconomic Status," *American Psychological Association*, http://www.apa.org/pi/ses/resources/publications/education.aspx.

that we need to direct our resources towards people who are different from ourselves. After the war in 1967, Israel and other nations began an active period of archeological exploration, particularly of Jerusalem. One of the interesting finds was that Jerusalem had a good part of town and an "other sides of the tracks" section. The good part of Jerusalem was located on the hill in the northern section of the city. The researchers discovered Greco-Roman homes that had commonly been owned by the wealthy. It appears that both Gentiles and Jews lived in this upscale neighborhood. The Tyropoeon Valley, translated as the "Valley of the Cheesemakers," separated this wealthy neighborhood from the poor section. The bad section ran from south of the temple to Gehenna (Valley of Hinnom). Rich citizens had to cross one of several bridges to enter the rougher section of Jerusalem. The rich man literally had to build or cross a bridge to help the poor.

Another clue lies in the word "perfect." Jesus says if we would be "perfect" we must sell our goods for the poor. This probably goes back to the Greek word *tam*. This word does not mean perfect in the way we understand it today. *Tam* actually means to be single-minded. If you would be single-minded in sharing love, this might be a way to understand this passage. Jesus may be asking us to do for others what we can based upon what we have.

Third, Jesus says, "sell your possessions." He did not say, "sell *some* of your possessions." This passage becomes very difficult if we go from "what I have" to "all I have." Such a proposition is definitely scary. It even seems unreasonable—after all, so many of us have children and responsibilities. If we sold everything, what would we do about tomorrow? Selling everything seems myopic. If I give everything away, who will take care of me? Following this passage is overwhelming, since even at the end of this lesson, this passage confronts us with a very difficult situation.

Closing

We must confess to God that this is too difficult for us. "I cannot do this; it is as impossible as it is for a camel to go through a needle's eye." We can take comfort in Jesus's final words: "with mortals this is impossible, and with God everything is possible." Maybe our sense of impossibility becomes fertile ground for God's possibility. When we do not rely on ourselves but rely instead on God, maybe all things are possible.

Discussion Questions

Who are the "rich"? America, most countries in Europe, Japan, Australia, and many other places are considered rich; how does this passage apply to us collectively, and it what ways might it not apply? What would it take for you to "sell everything"? How does being rich and being a good steward fit or not fit together?

4

Gnats and Camels

Opening Prayer

GRACIOUS HEAVENLY FATHER, WE thank you that you are a holy God. You are indeed most holy. Great is the majesty of your glory. As you are holy, you call us also to be a holy people. In that holiness, Father, grant that we may not lose sight of the holiness and wholesomeness of life, which is the lifeblood our existence. We ask this in Jesus's name. Amen.

Opening

Here is an old story you have probably heard before:

> There once was a schoolteacher, an unmarried woman who had saved up her pennies so that she could go to Paris. Of course, being a schoolteacher, she reached that goal. She had a wonderful time exploring the city, viewing the art, and browsing the boutiques. One evening, she decided to go to a very expensive restaurant. She ordered a seven-course meal and sat expectantly in the fancy restaurant. The first course was soup. When the soup arrived, she saw a dead fly floating in her bowl. She called to the waiter, "Waiter, there's a fly in my soup!" The waiter replied, "Mademoiselle, you are so lucky. Today the meat in the soup is free!"

Gnats and Camels

Today, we look at a little passage about tiny bugs and large camels "in our soup."

The Word

The lesson comes from the book of Matthew: "Woe to you, teachers of the law and Pharisees, you hypocrites! You give a tenth of your spices—mint, dill and cumin. But you have neglected the more important matters of the law—justice, mercy and faithfulness. You should have practiced the latter, without neglecting the former. You blind guides! You strain out a gnat but swallow a camel" (Matt 23:23–24). The emphasis here is on contrasting the heavier matter—the camel—in comparison with the a lighter matter—the gnat.

*Thinking of your own life, what are some
lighter matters and what are the heavier concerns?*

Make a list on the board.

*Ask yourself how much of your time and effort
go into the lighter matters.*

We will concentrate on two specific ideas: "tithing" and "straining out." First, let us look at tithing. Matthew accuses the Pharisees of paying strict attention to tithing while ignoring the weightier matters of the law. As Matthew notes, they pay close attention to dill and mint but not to justice and mercy. Tithing, according to the Old Testament, is the people's responsibility. It is not an option. Tithing supports the temple. Without tithing, there would be no temple and no priestly class. Without this income, there would be no worship. Just as with a modern church, it takes a certain amount of funding to pay the pastor, keep the lights on, and make sure the buildings are maintained. If Matthew is criticizing tithing, how is the temple supposed to operate?

The next idea is straining out. A commentator on Matthew named Luz,[1] points out that in the Old Testament there is a long list of what Jews should not eat. One of the things Jews are not supposed to eat is insects. Insects are unclean. In the ancient world, this was quite difficult. If one were to pour out a glass of wine and let it sit for more than a few minutes, some insects would likely begin to swarm around the wine. Pious Jews concerned about ritual purity would take the wine and strain it to ensure there were no bugs. Please note that for the pious Jew, straining the wine was a necessity in order to comply with dietary laws. Here again, in a sense, Matthew is not being fair to the Jews. He is pointing at that practice as if it were frivolous and silly.

As we move on, let us ask the question: To whom was this passage addressed? In Jesus's day, obviously, it was to the religious leaders. Jesus is specifically targeting those who are concerned with religious purity. Of course, we must remember that when Matthew was writing his Gospel (around 85 CE), he was not writing to Jews but to the early Christian community.

This passage leaves us with several questions:

- Is Matthew fair to the Jews?

As we will see, Matthew, more than any other gospel writer, portrays the Jews, and the Pharisees in particular, in a strongly negative light.

- What was Matthew warning Christians against?

Matthew retargeted the passage, turning it from focusing on the Jews and shifting it towards the Christians.

Ask the class's opinion.

The Context

The twenty-third chapter of Matthew is composed of a series of Jesus's sayings. Matthew placed the sayings into one chapter as a

1 See Ulrich Luz, *Matthew 8–20*, Hermeneia: A Critical & Historical Commentary on the Bible (Minneapolis: Fortress, 2001).

convenient and effective way of communicating the important utterances from Christ. We see the same thing in the several other chapters in Matthew (Matt 5–7, 10, 18, 24–25).

Many of the sayings in the twenty-third chapter are the "woe to you" statements. Matthew has Jesus uttering the phrase "woe to you" seven times, although those exact words occur nowhere else. This suggests that the "woe to you" structure Matthew created in the twenty-third chapter was his way of communicating this information. As we have noted, there are other places where Matthew clearly composed the sayings of Jesus. The repeated pattern indicates a strong effort to compose and not merely report the sayings of Jesus.

Scholars note that Matthew, more than any of the other gospel writers, was particularly unfair to Judaism. Matthew does not present a fair and balanced view of Judaism but rather skews it to focus on the worst and probably least common practices of the time. The chapter creates a caricature of the Pharisees. This caricature of the Pharisees is so popular that it has lasted to this day. This obvious slant supports the idea that Matthew composed the sayings of Jesus to make a specific point.

ℰℭ

The Q tradition

Common material found in Matthew and Luke, but not in Mark, has led scholars to suggest a common source for both Matthew and Luke. This common source is called the Q source (*Quelle* is German meaning "source"). According to this idea, Q was based on the collected saying s of Jesus from the oral tradition of Jesus's followers. Q is commonly, but not universally, accepted by Bible scholars.

ℰℭ

Any balanced look at the Pharisees would reveal that they made important and enduring contributions to the survival of Judaism. It is important to remember that after the destruction of the temple in 70 CE, the Pharisees were the religious leaders that carried on the practice of Judaism for thousands of years. The Pharisees were the entrepreneurial class of Palestine. They were business people, particularly in Jerusalem. Like many other business people, they were smart, they paid attention, and they were intelligent. They were the innovators of the economy of the time. Furthermore, if you look at Jesus's anger in the twenty-third chapter, he is angry at the entire religious institution. Remember, Jesus was a Jew, not a Christian. It is hard to imagine that a good practicing Jew like Jesus would be angry at every single aspect of Judaism.

For all these reasons, Matt 23 is probably a composition of Matthew. This is not to say that Matthew just made these things up. Rather, this suggests Matthew organized and inserted particular words or phrases in order to create this twenty-third chapter. Much of the material in Matt 23 also appears in the Q tradition. Remember that Matthew is composed largely of material found either in Mark or in material from the Q tradition. Matthew is not making material up, but he is stitching together the various materials from these two major sources to create a narrative of the life of Christ as the great teacher.

What is your response to the idea that Matthew "stitched together" a collection of Jesus's sayings? Does this mean these words somehow become less valuable?

If we accept that Matt 23 is a composition, it is also a polemic against Judaism. Why would Matthew, presumably a Jew, target Judaism? Let us look at Matt 13:52: He said to them, "Therefore every scribe of the law who has become a disciple in the kingdom of heaven is like the owner of a house who brings out of his storeroom new treasures as well as old."

Some scholars have suggested that Matthew was a scribe who had been converted to the Jesus movement. As a convert, he tried to win over his fellow scribes, and presumably many of them rejected him. It is possible that these scribes saw Matthew as a traitor and Jesus as a blasphemer. Since Matthew saw the "light," he began to assume that these other scribes were "blind." They were stubborn because they willfully ignored what was in front of them. This is one explanation for why the twenty-third chapter of Matthew seems so vitriolic.

Does it make sense that Matthew would target fellow Jews because they did not convert to the Jesus movement?

What Does It Mean for Us?

Matthew was warning the early Christians against a focusing on the exact details of the holy and ignoring the larger issues in the ordinary. Matthew is warning Christians not to become so fixated on one side (strict compliance) that they neglect the other side (justice). The camel and the gnat, as a heavier object and a lighter object, illustrate how we can become so concerned about the lighter concerns that we ignore the heavier ones. One can end up swallowing the camel by being a stickler for what is light, a gnat.

We can conclude, then, that Jesus was not concerned about religious "practice" but was concerned about religious "fixation." Jesus is warning against a fixation on "holiness." Here we must tread softly and avoid being judgmental. Let us try to look at fixation as just a phenomenon of the church, casting no judgment about whether it is right or wrong.

We can draw from our observations as active church people a phenomenological construct (a way of observing certain behaviors without casting judgment). It is certainly quite possible that you, the reader, will see things differently.

We have used the following graphic to communicate this phenomenological construct:

Draw this on the board:

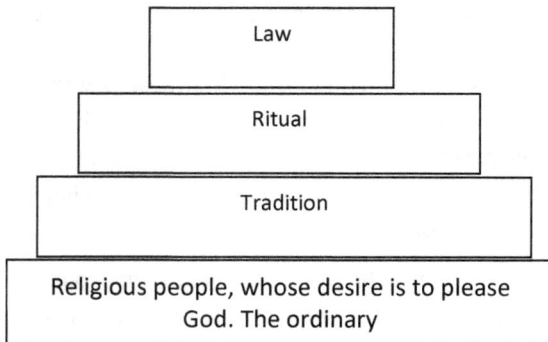

Law

Ritual

Tradition

Religious people, whose desire is to please God. The ordinary

The average religious person lives in a world where they do ordinary things. We buy groceries, clean our homes, visit friends, take care of our children, buy snacks for the soccer team, and let the neighbors' kids come over to play with ours. We live perfectly ordinary lives. For some religious people, these ordinary lives are not considered the arena for the holy. The holy lies somewhere else. Typically, people create arenas where holiness can be more fully and obviously played out, since the ordinary is not seen as the holy.

Tradition becomes one place where the holy manifests itself. For example, it is a tradition that Holy Communion should be offered by a member of the clergy. Some churchgoers have said that if they receive communion from someone other than a clergy member, it is not holy. Somehow, the minister makes the sacramental elements more than just ordinary things. This tradition goes back to the early days of the Christian church. We see holiness in this tradition.

Ritual is another way of setting the holy apart from the ordinary. An example of ritual comes from some Episcopal churches that offer communion with a common cup. At the end of the service, the priest must drink what is left in the cup. Of course, this can be a problem if there is too much wine left in the cup. To complete the ritual, the priest then pours a little water in the cup, swirls it around, and drinks it down. Finally, the priest dries the cup with a cloth napkin. The priest performs all of these ritualized steps to avoid leaving some of the sacred wine, now Jesus's blood, in the cup. It is not that the ritual is wrong, but the ritual sets apart the holy as separate from the ordinary. Ordinarily, people do not go through this kind of process when they enjoy a glass of wine.

Ask yourself as a congregation: What are the "holy" areas?
What are the special areas that must not be changed,
reviewed, or challenged? Again, thinking about your own
congregation, what is the balance of effort between
activities in the "holy" and the "ordinary?"

Law sets the holy apart from the ordinary. In the American South, blue laws decreed that certain entrepreneurial and economic behaviors could not occur on Sunday. The intent was to keep Sunday holy. For example, grocery stores would be closed on Sunday, as would auto parts stores and any other business deemed nonessential. You might buy your baby milk but not a baby bottle. The blue laws were enshrined as a part of Southern culture.

If tradition, ritual, and the law are the arenas for holiness, what are the arenas for justice, mercy, and faithfulness? It is in the ordinary that justice, mercy, and faithfulness exist. It is in ordinary life that these qualities play out. When Jesus talks about this, he says there is often so much concern about the light things, the holy things, that we neglect the weightier things. You should attend to both, he says. We must attend to both, not one or the other. The problem is that some religious folks become so fixated on the law and tradition that they lose sight of the ordinariness of life. The question then becomes, "What should be done in ordinary life?"

You might ask yourself, "Do justice and mercy occur in the law?" It is important to remember that Jesus was focusing on the Sabbath and dietary laws, not the laws governing ordinary, proper human behavior. In some ways, the entire Protestant revolution was about tearing down the wall between the holy and the ordinary. The ordinary *is* the holy, and the holy plays out in the ordinary.

There is a temptation to reduce the gospel to a series of do-and don't-statements. It is tempting to transform the gospel into a series of rules and regulations to live by. In such a case, we become like the Pharisees. Focusing on the gnats of holiness leads us to lose track of the camels of mercy and justice.

Why is it so tempting to reduce the full gospel into a series of dos and don'ts?

Let us look at three different examples and focus on how they illustrate religious fixation on holiness.

A young pastor went to teach a confirmation class. After teaching the class, the young pastor was called into the senior pastor's office. The senior pastor was preparing to leave the church because of a controversy about the common cup. The senior pastor insisted that the only legitimate way to serve Holy Communion was with the common cup. The senior pastor sat the young pastor down and proceeded to lecture him on why using the common cup was the only proper way to do things. For the senior pastor, this tradition had become an inviolate sanctuary of holiness.

There are many Christian traditions in which only immersion baptism is considered to really count as baptism. Sprinkling water on a child's head is not considered proper. There are some congregations that require people who were only sprinkled to be re-baptized the "proper way" by immersion.

There is an apocryphal story about several Russian priests. The priests were having a loud and heated discussion over the color of their stole. As these priests argued about whether this color or that color should be on the stole for a given festival, the Russian Revolution raged outside.

In all three stories, holiness is thought to be found in tradition and ritual. Tradition and ritual become more important than ordinary justice and mercy. We see the same process when we examine church doctrine.

We all know that Christians are split when it comes to Holy Communion. This is because we see the elements differently. Christian leaders in particular have argued vehemently over what happens to the elements. If there is a transformation, when does it happen, and how does it happen? Do the wine and bread become a real transformed substance, or are they strictly symbolic? These leaders are so caught up in questions of holiness that they lose sight of how we live with our brothers and sisters in Christ.

Here is another doctrinal issue we probably do not talk about often: in the Nicene Creed, there is a procession from the Father to the Son and so forth. The question is, does the Holy Spirit proceed from the Father and the Son, or does the Spirit proceed from the Father alone? Father and Son is the position of the Western church, and from the Father only is the position of the Eastern

Orthodox Church. For some religious leaders, this is a matter of life and death. People have actually died over this issue.

Let us talk about ethics. We all know that prior to the eighteenth amendment to the Constitution, slavery was a common practice in the United States. Many Southerners exerted significant effort to justify slavery based on holiness. The logic went something like this: these ignorant souls coming from the Dark Continent are damned unless we, the enlightened Christian souls, train them to become holy Christians. With this argument, slavery becomes a matter of eternal salvation and not economic exploitation.

Finally, many in the Christian church oppose homosexual relationships. When asked why, these Christians point to various passages in the Bible. The Bible becomes the justification. Is this a case of focusing on gnats while ignoring camels?

Closing

We would like to point out several challenges that we face as Christians. First, we need to be aware that a fixation on holiness exists. We need to recognize there is another dimension at play. Holiness is not just about specific religious practice but about how we operate in the ordinariness of life. Remember that it is in the ordinary that justice and mercy manifest themselves. We need to be opened to that other side, where those "other" people are residing. We need to open our ears to listen and learn from others' perspectives, lest our precise attention to holiness cause us to swallow the camel. Finally, we always need to seek out the essential heart of any other person's position. We must listen to the other person to hear what is most important in what he or she is saying. Then, based on listening to the "other" and the gospel, we can form a response.

Discussion Questions

How do you decide what is a "gnat" and what is a "camel?" How do you—how do we—practice mercy, justice, and faithfulness in the ordinary life? In what ways does the church display the holy in the ordinary? How do we decide which traditions, rituals, and laws need to change and which need to stay?

5

Swords

Opening Prayer

HEAVENLY FATHER, YOU CALL us to be Christians in a world that can be threatening. Give us the encouragement and strength not to succumb to the comforts of compliance. Instead, Father, give us the wisdom and strength to challenge the accepted, accept the unacceptable, and to live as God would have us live. Amen.

Opening

Even the simplest passage in the Bible can become quite complex with a little examination. Let us take, for example, the classic Johnannian passage "Jesus wept." Word comes to Jesus that something has happened to Lazarus. Jesus stays where he is for four days. When he arrives, others tell Jesus that Lazarus is dead, and Jesus goes to the tomb, where the text says Jesus wept. The question is: Why did Jesus weep? We can imagine any number of reasons.

Take a few minutes to make a list of reasons why Jesus might weep. Here are some explanations we came up with:

- *Jesus loved Lazarus.*
- *Mary was weeping, so maybe Jesus was empathizing with Mary.*

- *Maybe Jesus was aware of the unbelief surrounding him.*

- *Jesus wept because he foresaw his own death, as some scholars have suggested.*

- *Jesus may have wept over the fate of all humanity, which is death, and not God's intent.*

Jesus may have wept for any or all of these reasons or for many others. Even the text that seems as simple as "Jesus wept" can become quite a puzzle.

The Word

Today's lesson looks at a passage where it appears Jesus might be encouraging his disciples to arm themselves for violence. The ultimate weapon in Jesus's day was the sword. The Roman army used a short sword called a gladius; it was the AK-47 of its day.

> Then Jesus asked them, "When I sent you without purse, bag, or sandals, did you lack anything?" "Nothing," they answered. He said to them, "But now if you have a purse, take it, and also a bag; and if you don't have a sword, sell your cloak and buy one. It is written: 'And he was numbered with the transgressors'; and I tell you that this must be fulfilled in me. Yes, what is written about me is reaching its fulfillment." The disciples said, "See, Lord, here are two swords." "That's enough!" he replied. (Luke 22:35–38)

This passage occurs in the upper room and, of course, we all know what happens in the upper room: Jesus shares the Last Supper with his disciples and confronts his betrayer. In the upper room, Jesus may have warned Peter of his upcoming betrayal. The upper room holds a dramatic and central place in the Lord's last days. Not all of Jesus's sayings in the upper room are as well-known as those we just listed; one of the lesser-known sayings has to do with a sword.

The upper room marks a turning point in the ministry of Christ. Before the scene in the upper room, Jesus cured the ill, preached, and taught in Galilee. Starting with his entry into Jerusalem, Jesus was now inexorably marching toward the cross. Let us think about "then" and "now" as we look at the passage. In this passage, Jesus talks about what he did in Galilee and what he is asking in Jerusalem. Consider the following questions about then and now.

Thinking about geography, ask the following questions:

- Where was Jesus when he sent out the disciples without purse, bag, or sandals?
  Galilee.

- Where is Jesus is located now?
  Jerusalem.

- Back then, what did Jesus say about provisions?
  Nothing.

- Now that they are in Jerusalem, what does Jesus say about provisions?
  That provisions are needed.

- Back then, how much danger was there?
  No danger.

- Now that they are in Jerusalem, how much danger is there?
  A sword is needed.

- Back then, what did they take on their journey?
  Nothing.

- Now, in Jerusalem, what do they need to take on their journey?
  Everything they can.

Thinking about this comparison between when the disciples were in Galilee and then in Jerusalem, we see Jesus encouraging them to buy a sword. The disciples reply that they have two swords and Jesus lets them know that is enough.

What does Jesus mean by the phrase "it is enough?"

*Does he mean that two swords will be plenty for
what they need to do?*

*Does he mean, "I do not want to hear any more
talk about swords!"?*

The interpretation of this passage speaks directly to the character of Jesus. Let us ask ourselves a question: Is Jesus a violent revolutionary? Here, we want a simple yes or no answer. We can make a case for Jesus being a revolutionary, but we also find evidence against Jesus being a revolutionary.

Ask the class, "Is Jesus a violent revolutionary?"

A case can be made for and against Jesus being a violent revolutionary:

Yes, Jesus is a revolutionary	No, Jesus is not a revolutionary
• Jesus associated with sinners, not religious leaders.	• Jesus sends his disciples out as "lambs."
• Jesus does not keep all the Sabbath regulations.	• Jesus sends out his disciples to heal, not fight.
• Jesus appears unconcerned about ritual purity.	• When he is not welcome, Jesus tells the disciples to leave, not to pull out a sword.
• The people hailed Jesus as a king on Palm Sunday, and he did not dispute them.	• At his betrayal, Jesus heals a servant of the high priest.
• Jesus cleanses the temple; he was interested in giving a prophetic sign that the temple was on the verge of destruction.	• In the garden, Jesus tells his disciples to put away their swords.
• Jesus and his disciples often went to the Mount of Olives, which was historically associated with plotters.	• Jesus clearly states he is there not to change the law but to fulfill the law.
• Jesus dies on the cross, which, from the Roman point of view, means he was a revolutionary.	• Jesus encourages his followers to pray for those who repress them.

By calling people to return to the will of God, Jesus is being revolutionary, but it is not a violent revolution. If we think of Jesus as a revolutionary, then his statement to "buy a sword" represents him as a revolutionary challenging the government and fomenting change. If Jesus was not a violent revolutionary, as much of the New Testament suggests, then what does Jesus mean when he says to his disciples, "buy a sword?"

The Context

One way to resolve the issue of this "buy a sword" comment is to propose that the sword was not a literal sword but rather a figurative sword. "Sword" was a word intended to mean something else. Early church leaders advocated for the idea that the sword was a metaphor.

The early church developed what is called the "two swords doctrine." For a doctrine to be supported, there must be widespread biblical support, so early church scholars began to scour the New Testament to see if there were other passages that included two swords. The church scholars first looked at chapter 13 of Romans:

> Let everyone be subject to the governing authorities, for there is no authority except that which God has established. God has established the authorities that exist. Consequently, whoever rebels against the authority is rebelling against what God has instituted, and those who do so will bring judgment on themselves. For rulers hold no terror for those who do right, but for those who do wrong. Do you want to be free from fear of the one in authority? Then do what is right and you will be commended. For the one in authority is God's servant for your good. But if you do wrong, be afraid, for rulers do not bear the sword for no reason. They are God's servants, agents of wrath to bring punishment on the wrongdoer. Therefore, it is necessary to submit to the authorities, not only because of possible punishment but also as a matter of conscience. (Rom 13:1–5)

This passage justifies government as an extension of God's will and notes that when the state uses the "sword," it is as an instrument of God's will. Kings, queens, and other leaders used this passage to justify whatever punishment they deemed appropriate. As monarchs, they ruled as God's governmental representative and were only answerable to God; this was called the divine right of kings, and it was the dominating justification of government for over fifteen hundred years. The Romans passage puts forth that the state uses the "sword" to do God's will. There is another sword text in the New Testament: "For the word of God is alive and active. Sharper than any double-edged sword, it penetrates even to dividing soul and spirit, joints and marrow; it judges the thoughts and attitudes of the heart. Nothing in all creation is hidden from God's sight. Everything is uncovered and laid bare before the eyes of him to whom we must give account" (Heb 4:12–13).

This is a different kind of sword. This sword divides. This sword exposes corruption to the light. God gives us this sword to expose truth. In the Middle Ages, the Roman Catholic Church took the two swords passage from Luke and tied it in with the sword passages from Romans and Hebrews. The Roman Catholic Church put these together to create a doctrine that is called the "two swords doctrine." One sword was the sword that God put into the hands of the church to reveal the truth. The other sword, as we already noted, was in the hand of monarchs.

The two swords doctrine started in the early Roman Catholic Church but is now widely accepted across many Christian denominations. The two swords doctrine allows the church to use the sword to uncover heresies. From the two swords doctrine came the various Inquisitions and all the horrors that flowed from them. The church, wielding the sword of truth, could root out heretics that threatened the faith. Once the church uncovered a heretic, it turned that heretic over to the government for appropriate punishment. The church could use torture in search of truth and heresy, and the government punished the guilty. In this way, the church could stay free of the bloodguilt. The government wielded the sword of punishment as a way to ensure that subjects worked and lived together as the monarch thought best. Could it be that Jesus was talking about the two swords doctrine?

What do the participants think?

We argue that the answer is no. There are several reasons why it has to be no. First, in the passage Jesus is not addressing church and governmental leaders; he is speaking to his twelve disciples. Additionally, the Christian church was not yet created when Jesus spoke of buying a sword. Remember that Jesus was a practicing Jew. We must not create an anachronism by inserting something modern into a text that is ancient. Third, the two swords statement is really just a small aspect of Jesus's more important emphasis on how the disciples should behave now, as compared to when they were in Galilee. Finally, there is no evidence of the disciples acting violently. If we look through the book of Acts, we find no examples where the disciples pulled out a sword, opposed the government, or incited a crowd towards violence. Acts records no examples of the disciples acting violently in the face of persecution, arrest, and even death. This lack of violence suggests that the disciples did not understand the statement about two swords as a call to arm themselves.

We suggest that the early church fathers misunderstood this passage. If the two swords doctrine is not Jesus's point in talking about two swords, then what is the answer? It helps to remember that Jesus is speaking to his most loyal and faithful friends. The speech in the upper room is not a sermon but rather a conversation with those he loved and who loved him. We suggest that Jesus may be saying to his friends that the halcyon days of the early stage of his time on earth were ending. Harder days were ahead of him, and soon the hardest day of all would be upon them. Jesus could be telling his friends that the time of persecution and opposition could be upon them, and they better be prepared for that.

If Jesus is being figurative with his talk of swords, then why did he use that wording? Why did Jesus not just say, "Be prepared for opposition"? We must recall that the sword was a common part of the Roman world. The disciples had two with them in the upper room. The sword was the tool of division and opposition. Nobody in Jerusalem would have seen the sword as simply a tool of war. The sword as a harbinger of division is a common image in the Bible. Therefore, when Jesus tells them to prepare and buy a sword, he was trying to communicate that opposition and danger lay ahead. Like so many other times, the disciples misunderstood him and proudly held aloft their two swords.

What Does It Mean for Us?

Today we have few swords. Swords are displayed in museums as representing some historical past as tools of war. So what can we, as Christians in the twenty-first century, understand Jesus to be saying to us with this passage?

Today, Christianity is both encouraged and tolerated under specific conditions. Christianity is tolerated unless it upsets the cultural climate. During the great struggle that was the Civil War, many Christians called for slaves to be freed, while others called for slavery to be allowed to stay. Freedom for slaves upset the cultural standards of the antebellum South. When Christians called for segregation to end, Christianity upset the culture. Christianity is fine, as long as it stays in its place. When many Christians called for equality for homosexuals in matters of faith and law, it upset the cultural standards.

When Jesus warns the disciples to get ready for the fight in times to come, he may be speaking to all Christians, telling us to be prepared to stand against the culture and to speak the truth of the gospels. Is it the role of the Christian church to confirm and affirm the cultural standards, or does Christianity by its nature call us to division and strife between the world God would have us live in and the world we do live in? The moment we see Christianity as the bedfellow for our culture, we make a mistake. Christianity is not a bedfellow with the American way of life. Christianity is not a bedfellow with American capitalism. Christianity is not a bedfellow with the American way of democracy. Underneath, Christianity is prickly—it is thorny. Jesus may be saying in a manner, "Where you are, no matter where you live, do not get too comfortable. You may need a sword. You may need to fight."

Closing

In the passage about two swords, we are stuck on one central point. What was the character of Jesus? If he was a violent revolutionary, then his talk of swords is an active call to fight and to engage in violence. There is no shortage of examples of the Christian church using violence. From widespread violence like the wars of the Crusades to personal violence such as the torture of the Inquisition, the church has used the sword. If Jesus was not a man of violence but was "the Prince of Peace," then the sword is figurative. We think it is a call for Christians to stand outside the particular culture and act within the will of God. What do you think?

Discussion Questions

Does the current church still have and use a "sword"? What place should the church have when the state uses the sword? In what ways does the church continue the revolution?

How do we, as Christians, stand outside the American culture?

6

Judgment and Anger

Opening Prayer

HEAVENLY FATHER, WE KNOW that there are barriers in our lives between us and you, and between us and one another. We pray that where there are barriers, we may witness so that your good and gracious nature will be seen through us. Amen.

Opening

Today, our text will be Matt 5:21–26. In looking at this passage, we will be doing some very detailed analysis of what exactly is being articulated.

Let us begin by asking a question: Is anger bad or good?

Discuss among yourselves.

Obviously, if anger causes war, murder, or other forms of harm and destruction, then anger is bad. However, can evil anger be good?

Sometimes, anger can be good if it promotes some kind of change. In the past, both of the authors of this book have lost jobs because of financial exigencies or because of a lack of proper degrees and certifications. Losing those jobs made us very angry, but that anger also led both of us to finish our advanced degrees. We can suppose that in this case, the anger we felt motivated us toward something good.

Does the end justify the means?

Much evil has come from the ends justifying the means. The Holocaust, possibly the worst human rights tragedy of the twentieth century, was only intended as a step towards a wonderful end.

The Word

You have heard that it was said to the people long ago, "You shall not murder, and anyone who murders will be subject to judgment." But I tell you that anyone who is angry with a brother or sister will be subject to judgment. Again, anyone who says to a brother or sister, "Raca," is answerable to the court. And anyone who says, "You fool!" will be in danger of the fire of hell. Therefore, if you are offering your gift at the altar and there remember that your brother or sister has something against you, leave your gift there in front of the altar. First go and be reconciled to them; then come and offer your gift. Settle matters quickly with your adversary who is taking you to court. Do it while you are still together on the way, or your adversary may hand you over to the judge, and the judge may hand you over to the officer, and you may be thrown into prison. Truly I tell you, you will not get out until you have paid the last penny.

—MATT 5:21–26

Looking at the passage carefully, does it appear that Jesus believes that anger can be a productive emotion motivating us to change and to make things better?

Let us consider this passage carefully. What is the first clear statement Jesus is making? Looking at all of verse 21 and the first part of 22, it is clear that Jesus is saying, "Formerly not murdering was OK, but today I am telling you . . ." Jesus is comparing what the ancients said with what he, Jesus, says. The ancients said, "You shall not murder." However, Jesus says, "You shall not be angry." For Jesus, those who give in to anger subject themselves to the same judgment as those who murder. This is not a big deal for those of us who have never been angry. Unfortunately, every one of us stands under judgment for being angry.

Let us continue with this text. Besides speaking out against murder and anger, Jesus goes on to make several other points. Look at the text carefully to understand what these items are.

Besides condemning murder, what did the ancients say?

Jesus goes on to show that insults (verbal anger) lead to judgment. The judgment may be under the council, or it may be hellfire (*Gehenna*). Verbal insult brings judgment. An interesting translation problem arises in verse 22. *Raca* is most often translated into "fool." If so, the passage would read, "Again, anyone who says to a brother or sister, 'Fool' is answerable to the court. And anyone who says, 'You fool!' will be in danger of the fire of hell." How can saying "fool" bring about court judgment, and yet then saying "fool" puts one in hell? This is confusing. There are several unanswerable questions. Is Jesus implying some difference in degree between these ways of calling a person a fool? Is this part of Matthew's compositional style?

Following the verse about calling people *raca*, Jesus offers two examples. Both examples speak to the fundamental issue of reconciliation. The first has to do with worship. If a man (only men entered the temple at that time) were to go to the temple with a gift to place in front of the altar, then before he could present that gift, he would need to reconcile with the person who has something against him. In the second instance, if one were on the way to court, then one had better come to a compromise with the complainant. Without a compromise, the defendant ends up in jail. Once in jail, the defendant will not leave until the "last penny" is paid,

Note what Jesus does. He radicalizes the law. Not only murderers are under judgment—everyone who has ever been angry is under judgment. Notice also that he interiorizes the law. The sin is found not just in displays of anger (angry acts) but actually lies in how one feels on the inside. Jesus both radicalizes the foundation of judgment and also places people's interior feelings on equal footing with their exterior behavior.

The Context

Over the years, as you might imagine, people have tried to moderate what Jesus says in this text. The passage clearly puts all of us under judgment if we have ever been angry. Some scholars have tried to soften this interpretation. There are several ways the church, throughout the centuries, has tried to ameliorate or moderate the harshness of this passage.

Let us look at Matt 5:22: "But I tell you that anyone who is angry with a brother or sister will be subject to judgment. Again, anyone who says to a brother or sister, 'Raca,' is answerable to the court. And anyone who says, 'You fool!' will be in danger of the fire of hell."

Some translations put a footnote beside the word "angry" because some manuscripts of Matthew include the phrase "without cause" inserted after the word "angry." Remember, there are over four thousand individual manuscripts of the Gospel of Matthew. The passage changes from being "angry" to being "angry without cause."

How do we know when we are "justified" in being angry?

The majority of translations do not use the phrase "without a cause" in this passage. While it does exist in some manuscripts, the "better" manuscripts do not include this phrase. It is, therefore, difficult to point to this particular phrase as a way to wiggle out from underneath this judgment.

Now, let us look at Eph 4:26: "In your anger do not sin: Do not let the sun go down while you are still angry." The Ephesians passage allows us to be angry until "the sun goes down," which suggests that we should not hold a grudge or hold on to anger until the next day. This implies permission to be angry for a day; however, when the sun goes down, we need to let go of our anger. This passage allows us to wiggle our way out of judgment. As long as you are not angry for days on end, you are not under judgment. The problem is that Jesus is clear and Matthew is explicit, and it is only much later that the author of Ephesians throws in this caveat.

Some scholars have suggested that it is acceptable to verbally express anger as long as you do not express that anger physically. The verbal expression of anger is not a sin, but the physical manifestation of anger—violence—is. The problem is that in the Matthew passage, Jesus explicitly talks about verbal anger. Righteous anger is also a source of amelioration. Righteous anger stems from individuals who hold a morally superior position. Many people point to the story of Jesus in the temple as an example of righteous anger. It appears, some argue, that Jesus became quite angry in the temple when he overturned the table of the money changers. Yet the only problem with pointing to the example of Jesus and the money changers is that the word "anger" is never used. We might imagine that Jesus was angry at the money changers, but the text itself does not indicate that he was angry. Many horrible acts have been carried out under the supposed justification of righteous anger. Remember that the terrorists who attacked the World Trade Center likely used righteous anger as an excuse to justify their cowardly actions. Righteous anger becomes a cloak to cover anything we want to do. Keeping all this in mind, interpretations that rely on righteous anger must fall by the wayside.

Psychology offers another way to moderate Jesus's words. People have argued that anger is a fundamental part of human nature. Indeed, the emotion of anger is an honest and common part of who we are as humans. To be a human being is to feel anger. In that case, it seems angry feelings are OK, but anger becomes a sin when its expression manifests through violence.

Maybe anger can serve as motivation to make changes. For example, people who were angry that homeless people were hungry started our local food bank. We, as human beings, can imagine many ways in which anger can motivate us to some greater good. Yet Jesus's words remain clear: if you are angry, you are under judgment.

Sometimes, we as a people will play a word game, substituting different words for "angry" in the hope of changing the text's meaning. For example, we can use the word "concerned" as a replacement for anger. Apparently, if we are concerned, we are not angry. There are probably many words we could use to replace "anger" like "indignant" or "aggravated." Does the word game really work? Unfortunately, no matter how we play with this phrase, no matter how many words we may substitute, we remain with Jesus's declaration that if you are angry, you are under judgment. Here is a list of conclusions we feel confident making about this passage:

- Jesus does not look at anger in terms of practicality.
- Jesus does not look at anger in terms of chronology.
- Jesus does not view anger in terms of psychology.
- Jesus does not see anger as a clever word game.
- Jesus does not look at anger in terms of what is internal and what is external.

There are many instances in the Bible where God seems to be angry with his people. We could point to Noah and the flood as a possible story of God's anger. Since God can be angry with us, is it OK for us to be angry, as God appears to be? This is an interesting question. Of course, there is danger in thinking we can be like God. All these ways of moderating the text ultimately fall short. The question is: Why is Jesus so harsh?

Any thoughts?

What Does It Mean for Us?

Jesus understands anger in terms of God's will. God's will is that there should be no anger. Anyone who feels anger is under God's judgment. Before going further, we need to look at the assumptions behind Jesus's statement. In stating that to be angry is to be under judgment, it seems Jesus understood something about us as humans:

1. Jesus assumes that everyone is under judgment because everyone gets angry.

2. Jesus assumes that his followers, like himself, will want to do God's will.

3. Jesus assumes, therefore, that his followers will be working towards feeling no anger. *Note that Jesus tells people that before worship, they should reconcile. Note also that when he talks about court, Jesus encourages us to settle. In these examples, Jesus assumes that his workers will strive towards feeling no anger. In the Lord's Prayer, we all pray "thy will be done." We all seek to do the Lord's will.*

4. Finally, Jesus does not condemn efforts that fail. *These examples do not condemn. Rather, through these examples, Jesus tried to encourage his followers to move towards feeling no anger.*

Jesus clearly knows that it is human nature to feel and show anger. It is interesting to think about what human nature truly is. Is human nature the nature we saw in the garden, when humankind lived in communion and fellowship with God? Maybe human nature is the nature we saw after the fall of Adam. If we think of Jesus as an example of human nature, then what is human nature? Is Jesus's human nature the same as the broken and faulty nature we share? Jesus's nature could be the pre-fall human nature—a human nature that lives in companionship with the eternal God.

What is human nature? As people who have lived in the world, we all have assumptions about what it means to be a human.

The text suggests things we can do to move towards feeling no anger. The passage concerning verbal abuse and calling people names like a "fool" or "fuzzy head" suggests that self-control might be important. We do not often call people fools, despite frequent our desire to do so.

Are there any options available to help us limit or control our self-expression? Shutting up, walking away, taking a break, attending a class on anger management, and improving our communication skills are all tools that can help us move towards a place of feeling no anger.

Let us look at reconciliation again. Who is reconciled to whom? The person who has committed the offense is the one who can initiate reconciliation. This is clearly difficult to do, but we can all reconcile ourselves to those we have offended when we are in the wrong. If we are at fault, we are responsible for cleaning up our own mess.

Where does compromise fit? We have many ways to argue, confront, and even attack people. Today in Congress, "compromise" appears to be a dirty word; attack with no room for surrender seems to be much more the tone these days. Unfortunately, this lack of compromise has put us in a difficult position.

It is important to remember that with all these measures, God is at work. If it is God's intent that there should be no anger, then God is willing to contribute mightily to make that happen.

Where does grace exist in this passage? We see grace in lots of areas. Grace is in the fact that we have the power to initiate reconciliation. Grace is in the community resources that are available to us. In our community of believers, we can practice our skills. In the larger community, there are many groups—Alcoholics Anonymous, for example—where we can learn to reconcile ourselves to those we have wronged.

How can our church community help us to move
towards the "no anger" area?

Closing

Remember that when we fail, God takes us up, dusts us off, pats us on the back, and sends us on our way. God cares that we keep moving towards a "no anger" world. God's grace can be seen in the Holy Spirit that works within us so that God's will can be carried out.

Jesus is harsh. Jesus says there is to be no anger. As authors, we think that Christians should not try to wiggle out from that expectation. When we Christians struggle to move toward a life of "no anger," we can perhaps begin to see the power that feeling no anger gives us. We can see that God is actually empowering us—and through us, our communities—by helping us to overcome anger. That is a remarkable achievement. Amen.

Discussion Questions

Are there some practical steps you can take to move toward becoming a "no anger" person?

Is there a danger to suppressing anger? Anger is often described as a second feeling. We experience anger *after* feeling something else first. What are some common feelings that lead to anger? What steps can you take to make your congregation a "no anger" place?

7

Getting Even

Opening Prayer

GRACIOUS HEAVENLY FATHER, WE live in a world that is full of retaliation, and we pray that when we are hurt by others, you will give us the grace, courage, and determination to not get even. As difficult as that may be, grant us, heavenly Father, that we may press towards the greater good, not only for ourselves but also for those who are our adversaries. We ask this in Jesus's name. Amen.

The Word

The passage for today is Matt 5:38–42:

> You have heard that it was said, "Eye for eye, and tooth for tooth." But I tell you, do not resist an evil person. If anyone slaps you on the right cheek, turn to them the other cheek also. And if anyone wants to sue you and take your shirt, hand over your coat as well. If anyone forces you to go one mile, go with them two miles. Give to the one who asks you, and do not turn away from the one who wants to borrow from you.

After reading this passage, many think the general tone of this passage is one of revenge. There is a vengeful attitude here. Despite the many times this passage is cited as justification for revenge, in its original context, the passage had little to do with revenge; rather, it had to do with justice. In ancient societies, bloodguilt was seen as justice. If one person committed a crime against another person, the offended person (or their clan or tribe) could lawfully seek revenge against the perpetrator. For example, if a man from one tribe stole a horse from another tribe, the victim could kill the thief's son. It was a real Hatfields-and-McCoys sense of justice. This was all done to seek bloodguilt. There was no sense of balance between the crime and the punishment.

The Context

After a long stretch of human history, people began to realize that there ought to be something called equivalent justice. If one person wrongs another, the offended person cannot do whatever they like to get revenge. There needs to be equivalence between the offense and the revenge. Rulers, kings, and courts began to wrestle with this idea of equivalence. In fifth-century Greece, Aeschylus wrote the *Oresteia* as a trilogy of Greek tragedies on the theme of revenge. The first play in the trilogy is entitled *Agamemnon*. Agamemnon, King of Argos, returns from the Trojan War only to be immediately killed by his wife, Clytemnestra. In the trilogy's second play, *The Libation Bearers* (Χοηφόροι), Electra and Orestes, Agamemnon's children, seek revenge against their mother for murdering their father. Orestes kills Clytemnestra to avenge the death of Agamemnon. In the third and final play, *The Eumenides,* a trial completes the chain of tragic events that started with the original murder. Athena prepares to judge Orestes for the murder of Clytemnestra, but due to the many extenuating circumstances, Athena sets up a court instead of having the Furies pounce on Orestes and drag him into torment. Athena, together with eleven judges she selects from among the Athenians, decide whether the son's choice to kill his mother made him guilty of murder. This story illustrates that ancient Greeks were struggling with the idea of equivalence and punishment.

Ancient Hebrews also struggled with this idea of equivalence. Looking at the nineteenth chapter of Deuteronomy, we see the first reference to the idea of revenge that will later show up in Matthew. But notice the reference is not about revenge for a crime:

> One witness is not enough to convict anyone accused of any crime or offense they may have committed. A matter must be established by the testimony of two or three witnesses. If a malicious witness takes the stand to accuse someone of a crime, the two people involved in the dispute must stand in the presence of the Lord before the priests and the judges who are in office at the time. The judges must make a thorough investigation, and if the witness proves to be a liar, giving false testimony against a fellow Israelite, then do to the false witness as that witness intended to do to the other party. You must purge the evil from among you. The rest of the people will hear of this and be afraid, and never again will such an evil thing be done among you. Show no pity: life for life, eye for eye, tooth for tooth, hand for hand, foot for foot. (Deut 19:15–21)

What is the context of this passage?

The context of this passage is a courtroom.

For whom is a punishment sought?

It is not sought against the perpetrator but against the false witness. If someone lies in court, they will receive the punishment that was directed towards the person on trial. In its original context the phrase, "eye for an eye" was not about revenge, but about equivalence. Despite the original intent, by the time of Jesus, the passage in Deuteronomy became about "tit for tat" retaliation. Imagine if you were a thief in the time of Jesus: if you stole bread, then your hand could be cut off in punishment. This is harsh, but better than death. After some time, money became a way of compensating for the damage done. For example, in early American history, if someone killed another person's child, the killer would have to pay the family the sum of money the child would have earned in the coming years. Whether the method is financial restitution or physical revenge, this notion of justice has to do with equivalent retaliation, tit for tat.

When Jesus says in Matt 5:39, "But I tell you, do not resist an evil person," he uses the word *anthistemi*, which means to set one's self against, to withstand, resist, or oppose. Of course, this Greek word *anthistemi* looks very much like our "antihistamine." We who suffer from hay fever know antihistamines all too well. An antihistamine resists the histamines that trigger allergic reactions. *Anthistemi* does not mean doing nothing. Notice that Jesus does not say, "do nothing" or "seek appropriate revenge." We are stuck with the phrase "do not resist." The question is: Does the translation "do not resist" reflect Jesus's intent?

*Is there any difference between resistance
and retaliation?*

Imagine that there is evil and that we do not resist it. Not offering resistance would mean letting evil have its way. But if we offer no retaliation, that does not mean evil has a free and clear passage. When we look at the examples found in this little passage, it becomes quite clear that Jesus is speaking of the way the law was being treated by the people of his day. That is, people in his day were reading the law as if justice were "tit for tat," or getting even. We believe that those listening to Jesus heard him challenging them to not seek revenge.

If that is true, then maybe we should read the verb *anthistemi* not as "do not resist" but as "do not retaliate." It calls us not to repay in kind those who have wronged us. If the verb means "do not retaliate," this leaves us with the option of resistance without retaliation. Jesus may not be saying "do not resist," but maybe Jesus is saying "don't pay back in kind," or "do not retaliate against one who comes at you forcefully." If Jesus allows us to resist without retaliating, then we can ask ourselves, "What type of resistance is permissible?" There are some clues within the text that may show us what resistance without retaliation looks like.

Reread the text and see if you can find the clues.

Did you find any clues? How are people in this text being described? At first, the people might seem passive. In each case the person is reacting. They are not getting even, but they do resist through their actions. The people are forcefully compelled to act, but they do not react in kind. They go beyond what is being forced on them. Likewise, a story is often told of a man who was mugged. After he gave the thief his wallet, he offered his coat, since it was a cold night. The victim went beyond what was demanded of him, and by going beyond what he was forced to do, he exemplified turning the other cheek. The victim did not just stand there; he did something. The story illustrates three points: First, victims must resist. Second, we resist, but we do not retaliate. Finally, this resistance moves us beyond the compulsion of force.

What Does It Mean for Us?

We think there are some noteworthy characteristics in the way Jesus calls us, as Christians, to react. First, our reaction to injustice should be non-retaliatory, whatever the initiator has done. Obviously, our reaction will be colored by the initiator's action. For example, if the initiator is being violent, then non-retaliation means to not retaliate or add to the violence. The initiator's wrongdoing does not give us permission to enter into the wrong.

Second, our response needs to be active, not passive. Jesus does not call us to do nothing but rather to resist the evil one's act. We are not to simply shrug and let evil have its way. We *do* react and respond, but we do not retaliate. Third, there is no reference in the text to success or effectiveness. Jesus offers us no guarantee offered of success in our resistance. For example, if we turn the other cheek, there's a chance that other cheek will get hit too. There is no guarantee that we will not get slapped again. That is pretty tough. As Americans, our mind-set is to do what works. If there is no guarantee that taking a non-retaliatory stance will "work," then why do we do it? We do it because we are commanded by Christ to do it. There are many Christian martyrs who gave their lives because they were commanded by Christ. They certainly resisted, but they did not seek revenge.

As with other difficult passages, people often attempt to avoid the harshness of this passage. The first attempt comes from psychology. Some scholars have noted that if we actively respond in the face of force, then in some small way we are not helpless victims. If we are asked to contribute $10 toward a work function and we give $15 instead, we are making a decision and not just following some inane office policy about birthday cakes. The boss may think he or she has the upper hand. If you slap me and I turn the other cheek, the initiative becomes mine and not yours. We do not think this is Jesus's main concern, however. We feel Jesus is clearly speaking to revenge when he says, "do not pay back in kind."

Another way to avoid the harshness of this directive is to suggest that maybe Jesus meant we should not retaliate toward *nonlethal* attacks. The implication is that we are allowed to retaliate or actively resist in face of *lethal* acts. It is not as if Jesus is asking us to allow someone to shoot us twice. To our ears, this may make sense. Jesus is not asking us to die, just not to seek revenge. Unfortunately, nothing in what Jesus says supports any such distinction.

What do you think?

Maybe another way to approach the issue is to think about defense versus offense. Maybe Jesus is calling upon us not to be offensive but to choose to be defensive instead. Many of the martial arts are focused less on attacking and more on defending against attacks from others. Ironically, the attacker creates the very energy this kind of martial artist uses to fend off their attack. Maybe this is what Jesus means—that we should resist *not* through offensive action but through defensive action.

What you think?

Recall the incident at the Edmund Pettus Bridge on March 7, 1965. Civil rights activists walked across the bridge on their historic march to Montgomery. The local sheriff, Jim Clark, ordered all local white men over the age twenty-one to report to the courthouse and be deputized. As the civil rights marchers crossed the bridge, these regular and irregular officers attacked them with clubs and police dogs. The marchers neither struck back nor ran away. Seventeen marchers were hospitalized, and at least fifty protestors were injured. Is this the kind of resistance Jesus meant? It is certainly possible that violence could be made worse by resistance. When threatened with the loss of power, those who are willing to use violence may increase the intensity of violence to retain their sense of power. There is simply no guarantee that the nonviolent resistance we believe Jesus calls for will change the hearts and minds of others or keep us safe.

Think about the passion of Jesus for a moment. Recall the moment when the soldiers came to Jesus in the garden and the disciples drew their swords.

৪০০৪

Herod Antipater, known as Antipas, was the ruler of Galilee during the time of Jesus. Antipas was raised in Rome in the court of Cesear Augustus. He is best known today for accounts in the New Testament of his role in events that led to the executions of John the Baptist and Jesus of Nazareth. That Jesus met Antipas is documented in the Gospel of Luke. No record exists of what transpired between Herod and Jesus. It is one of those things that would be interesting to know and is lost to history.

৪০ ৪৪

Jesus chastised the disciples to put their swords away. When Jesus arrived at the Sanhedrin, the Jewish Council, he was charged with many crimes and confronted with many false witnesses. Jesus offered no words. He did not challenge them or point out their failures. In other words, Jesus did not respond in kind. In one play, when Jesus goes to Herod, the king challenges Jesus to walk across some water or show him a miracle. In no way does Jesus respond. Eventually, Jesus arrives before Pilate. Pilate asked Jesus, "Are you king of the Jews?" Jesus only response is "That is what you say I am." Again, he does not argue, debate, challenge, or threat. On the cross, how does Jesus respond? Jesus responds by asking the Father to forgive the soldiers for their sins. At every location in the passion narrative, Jesus resists but does not retaliate.

Recall that Christians live in two kingdoms: one of the earth and one of heaven. One is broken and filled with sin, while the other is perfected. Remember that we, as Christians, stand in both kingdoms. We somehow must learn to live in a sinful and violent world, and yet we must act as if we live fully in the kingdom of God. Jesus calls us to not retaliate. We can and do respond, but we never respond by getting even.

Closing

Whether it is World War II or the terrorism at the World Trade Center, there often seems to be a "sensible" violent response to these injustices. Certainly, the Holocaust required a violent response, as did the attack on the innocents killed in the Oklahoma City bombing. However, Jesus says there should be no retaliation. Is Jesus's stance practical? In the kingdom of earth, it may not be practical. The problem is that as Christians, we also stand in the kingdom of God. In cases like these, we are stuck between those two kingdoms. We struggle with how to be citizens of the kingdom of God and yet live practically as citizens of the world. We are both holy and broken at the same time. The text is clear. The question is one we struggle with because there is no definitive answer. Like

Adam, we want everything, but are we willing to pay the full price of being citizens in the kingdom of God?

Discussion Questions

Does Jesus's admonishment against revenge apply only to interpersonal relations and not international relations, especially regarding wars and military action? What do you think Jesus would say about our current national debate about gun control? How does a parent spanking a child fit into Jesus's ideas of no retaliation? Many people think of retaliation as only a physical act, but can retaliation also include verbal responses, like screaming at someone with the intent of harming them?

8

It Is the Truth, I Swear

Opening Prayer

LORD, GRACIOUS GOD, WE come to you and ask that, just as the cool waters of a stream refresh the thirsty one, so may our speech with one another refresh us. In Jesus's name we pray. Amen.

Opening

Let us start with the experience of a high school student, the young Charlie Sigel. One of Charlie's teachers at his all-boys high school was John Wesley Rhoades. He was one of the few teachers who had a doctorate. Charlie admired him because at their all-boys school, where testosterone-levels often ran high, Dr. Rhoades was the model of Christian life. He ran a Bible study group that met after school.

Charlie was interested in drama, and had acted in a number of school plays. Charlie had even written a play of his own. Charlie had intended it to be a mystery play, but unfortunately the drama teacher turned it into a comedy. Charlie's play originally included many exclamations such as "My God," but Charlie had become a fundamentalist, so he wanted to avoid such exclamations, particularly if they involved God. Consequently, Charlie turned "My God" into "By heaven." After calmly explaining "By heaven" in class, Dr. Rhoades came to Charlie and pointed him towards a passage in the

Matt 5:33–37. Dr. Rhoades pointed to the passage from the Gospel of Matthew not to chide Charlie, but to advise him. Charlie's mentor intended to guide him towards a more godly life.

The Word

Again, you have heard that it was said to the people long ago, "Do not break your oath, but fulfill to the Lord the vows you have made." But I tell you, do not swear an oath at all: either by heaven, for it is God's throne; or by the earth, for it is his footstool; or by Jerusalem, for it is the city of the Great King. And do not swear by your head, for you cannot make even one hair white or black. All you need to say is simply "Yes" or "No"; anything beyond this comes from the evil one.

—MATT 5:33–37

Now, let us return to the story. Dr. Rhoades said to Charlie, "Mr. Sigel, you really should not have phrases like 'by heaven' and so on, because this passage says not to swear by either heaven, earth, or anything else." For Charlie, a young man with such high regard for Dr. Rhoades, there was only one thing to do: Charlie went through the play and took out all the oaths.

Dr. Rhoades was quite right in encouraging Charlie to avoid saying "My God" and replace it with something more acceptable. The text clearly says to not swear by these things. However, in terms of a larger issue in the text, we think Dr. Rhoades missed the main point.

Really read the text, and then ask yourself:
What is this larger issue?

As with other texts we have looked at, Jesus is comparing what the ancients said with what he is saying. A good first question then is: What did the ancients say? The ancients were saying that if you make a promise to God, you must fulfill it. This seems pretty specific and narrow.

Look at verse 34 and see what Jesus says. Jesus says to not swear at all. Jesus took this narrow and specifically focused admonition of the ancients and broadened it.

The ancients said	Jesus says
If you swear to God make sure to complete your promise	Do not swear on anything.

The word "swearing" is an interesting one. Swearing often means using foul language. We all know the vulgar words. Swearing is sometimes confused with cursing. Cursing can also mean using foul language. More accurately, a curse is an appeal (maybe a prayer) for evil or misfortune to happen to someone. For example, you can curse someone by telling them to "go to hell" or "I hope you die" or expressing a wish for some other terrible outcome. Jesus uses the word "swear" (*omnuo*) specifically; he refers to making an oath or promise. Jesus is not talking about cursing or foul language but about making a vow.

Now, look at verse 37. In verse 37, Jesus encourages his listeners to have their "yes" mean "yes" and their "no" mean "no." A common saying is "Say what you mean and mean what you say." Jesus adds that any swearing oaths comes from the evil one. Putting the two components together becomes a real challenge. Jesus tells us that we are not to swear and that any oath-taking beyond yes and no comes from evil. How many times do people carefully phrase what they say in order to confuse or deceive? What person doesn't lie on a daily basis? Even little white lies are included under Jesus's comments. For example, imagine that a husband steps out of his closet wearing two items that look hideous together and asks for his wife's approval. What wife would say, "You look awful"? It is more likely that his wife would tactfully direct her husband towards a shirt that actually matched his pants. We have all learned to be careful—even somewhat political—in what we say. We all know how to deceive, sometimes out of love and other times for lesser motives.

The Context

This text concerns the whole issue of trustworthy speech in a much larger way. Maybe there was a time in human history when men and women could say, "My word is my bond." Certainly, we have all met people whose handshake was a guarantee. Unfortunately, both historically and currently, there are more than enough people for whom even a guarantee is not really a guarantee. This issue of deception reaches all the way back to childhood. Remember the phrase "Cross my heart and hope to die?" Maybe this was an attempt, through some ritual, to say, "This time, unlike all the other times, you can really trust what I say." We all know the universal rule that crossing your fingers is supposed to negate any lie you may be telling, or at least that is what we thought when we were twelve. Even kids know the power of an oath—children know that such a vow is meant to communicate that some power is compelling the truth. This Matthian text goes much deeper than the concern Dr. Rhoades expressed. It is so much more than mere exclamations.

ဢဢ

Traditionally the evil
one is called many
names, some of which
follow: The Satan (a
functional title that
means prosecuting
attorney), Satan (a
proper name), the
serpent, Lucifer,
Beelzebub, Prince of
Darkness, Angel of
Light, Roaring Lion,
and the Dragon. Some
are biblical and some
are cultural. There is
no one understanding
of the "evil one."

ဢဢ

Let us now turn to the last phrase in verse 37.

Reread verse 37.

In Greek the word for evil, as found in verse 37, is *ponēros*. This word also appears in the Lord's Prayer: "lead us not into temptation and deliver us from evil [*ponēros*]." The phrase "evil one" is also frequently translated as just "evil." See what we have done: we have turned "evil one" into an abstract and not a devilish figure. For now, let us go with "evil one."

Ask yourself: What do you understand the "evil one" to be?

For most people, the evil one is understood as being Satan or the devil. The Bible tells us the devil is the father of lies: "You belong to your father, the devil, and you want to carry out your father's desires. He was a murderer from the beginning, not holding to the truth, for there is no truth in him. When he lies, he speaks his native language, for he is a liar and the father of lies" (John 8:44).

So if the passage from Matthew says, "from the evil one," and we understand the "evil one" to be the devil, then what is Jesus saying? Jesus says to let your "yes" be "yes" and your "no" be "no," and anything else is a lie from the father of lies. The devil is the source of oaths and vows.

Think about this passage: What is the implication here for how you live your life?

Now, if we don't think word *ponēros* means "the evil one" and believe instead that it just means "evil," this leads us to the idea of deception. We deceive people when we say anything more than our yes is yes and no is no. Social scientists see deception as a large category of behaviors and lying as one specific version of deception. When someone has misunderstood us and we allow them to continue in that misunderstanding—even just by not saying anything to correct them—this is a deception, but it is not a lie. When we tell someone the truth but couch it in misleading terms, that is deception, but that is not a lie. We even have different types of lies. We might say that something is a "bold-faced lie" or a "white lie." Politicians report "facts" they often know to be untrue, and yet they state them with conviction. That is a "political lie." We might even be lying for some greater good, such as when we tell our young children that there is a Santa Claus, Easter Bunny, or Tooth Fairy. Once we get into deception and lies, we open a giant can of worms.

Jesus seems to be saying that speech does not need props. Speech does not need oaths. Speech ought to be trustworthy in and of itself. This poses a great many problems. Think about the first passage of the Gospel of John: "In the beginning was the Word, and the Word was with God, and the Word was God" (John 1:1).

Notice the use of "word" here. Significantly, John's gospel says that in the beginning was the Word. From the beginning God intended to communicate. What, then, does God intend for our words to be?

What Does It Mean for Us?

It is a challenge to think about the role that deception and lying play in our lives. We may feel a deep desire for nostalgia—to recall a time when life seemed simpler. We can all recall times when people's word was as trustworthy and faithful as God's love: it may have been a salesperson who took a handshake for a business deal, a fellow Christian who promised to buy a house, or an adult who shook our mother's hand and came through on their promise to help. This deep nostalgic desire permeates so much of what we recall, but as social scientists point out, nostalgia involves "recall bias." That is, we tend to remember only the positive, while the mundane and ordinary fade into the fog of memory. Only when we examine the past with the cold, clear lens of a historical researcher do we recognize that the past is filled with just as much complication, lying, and deception as we have today.

"Obfuscation" is a wonderful word. It's not a word you hear often. It means to put a veil in front of what you're saying—to make something obscure or unclear. It seems that God meant communication, not obfuscation. We wonder if God is using Jesus as a model for communication to humanity. That is not in the text; nevertheless, it may be that Jesus is looking at God in terms of communication.

The way God speaks—faithfully and in a trustworthy way—is the way that we, as people, should speak to one another.

Notice that in the text, Jesus says we should not swear by heaven, Jerusalem, or even on our own heads. We think oaths may be a sign of human presumption. Notice the passage, "And do not swear by your head, for you cannot make even one hair white or black" (Matt 5:36). Jesus is pointing to our powerlessness. How can we swear by our heads when we cannot even control, without the help of many modern chemicals, the color of our own hair? When we call upon God, we are attempting to bind God to our word. We see this when people swear before God to tell the truth when they testify in court.

Can God be bound by our word?

Trying to call God to our side when we swear by something transitory, like our heart (as in "cross my heart") or a city, is presumptive. Cities are destroyed and hearts stop working, but God's love for his people endures forever.

There is a question of practicality here. Is Jesus's word a practical word? We have several reasons for raising this point. We live in a world where we are surrounded by oaths. Politicians swear to uphold the Constitution when they enter elected office. In some Christian colleges, professors are required to take an oath that they will follow the inerrant, infallible Word of God. Some professions require people to take oaths when they receive their license. Federal employees must take an oath when they begin their career. In court, people are occasionally asked to swear by God to tell the truth. All around us there are oaths. Surrounded as we are by vows, we are also surrounded by attempts to avoid the truth. From little "white lies" to great "big whoppers," we all are subject to so much lying. Think about our personal relationships: What would happen if we always told the truth? So the question stands: Was Jesus practical?

Closing

We suggest that you look at the Sermon on the Mount. This sermon is our call to live in the kingdom of God. The very first passage of the Sermon on the Mount specifically references the kingdom. Throughout the entire Sermon on the Mount, we find several references to the kingdom of God. It is clear that the entire sermon is directed towards living life within the kingdom.

We have two feet. Do we stand with both feet in the kingdom of God in our present day? We suggest that, as Christians, we stand with one foot in the kingdom of God and the other foot firmly in the world. As a human, Jesus experienced life between two locations: a broken world and the kingdom of God. Remember that Judas betrayed Jesus and that Peter denied him. Jesus was surrounded by untrustworthy speech. Yet his point is that speech should be trustworthy, as his was. When we prop up our speech with oaths, we indicate the falsity of what we normally say. Therefore Jesus swears no oaths. Because we have one foot in the kingdom and one foot in the world, we are called to offer as much trustworthy speech as we can possibly conjure up without props. Tempered by love, we need to speak as much truth as we can. The overarching principle that runs through this text is that *Jesus understands that the human community is enhanced by honest communication and not by devious obfuscation.* Of course, we will fail, and that failure drives us back to grace. Grace and grit are the key. Grace is knowing that God takes us up, and grit is the determination to do better next time.

Discussion Questions

How does the switch from "evil one" to "evil" change the passage for you? Is there a difference between lying and deception? How does Jesus radicalize the idea of swearing? Is lying for some higher good or purpose acceptable (as a means to an end)? What does it mean to live with one foot in the kingdom?

Appendix

Sermon on the Mount and the Antitheses

Opening Prayer

GRACIOUS GOD AND FATHER, we are often so engulfed in cloudy mist that we cannot always find our way. We ask, therefore, that in your grace, you will illuminate us with the light of your Word and thus direct us to do your good and gracious will. To the honor and glory of your holy name. Amen.

Theological Overview

In this lesson, we will do a quick theological overview of the Sermon on the Mount and the antitheses.

The Sermon on the Mount is composed of three chapters in Matthew's gospel: chapters 5, 6, and 7. In arranging the material in his gospel, Matthew likely took material from the Jesus tradition, including Jesus's own words, and wove it into the text we know as the Sermon on the Mount.

The Antitheses

The "antithesis" is a scholastic term given to a group of sayings enfolded within the Sermon on the Mount. They are the passages in which Jesus says, "You have heard it said . . . But I say . . . ." These are antitheses because Jesus sets himself over and against the traditions of the elders. This means the antitheses effectively show us the ways in which Jesus understands the interpretation of the law. Consequently, the antitheses portray how Jesus's followers should "live" the law. It is important to recognize that all of these antitheses describe general, conventional, social relationships.

It is significant that Jesus introduces the antitheses with a clear statement about the law: "Do not think that I have come to abolish the Law or the Prophets; I have not come to abolish them but to fulfill them. For truly I tell you, until heaven and earth disappear, not the smallest letter, not the least stroke of a pen, will by any means disappear from the Law until everything is accomplished" (Matt 5:17–18). The fulfillment of the law is very important. The fact that Jesus made such a strong statement about fulfilling the law suggests that in the antitheses we are seeing the way Jesus understands the antitheses.

The antitheses are examples of love in action. All the antitheses begin with an unspoken phrase. This phrase is not actually in the text, but if we were to read it, it would go something like this: "You have heard it said . . . but where love is . . . ." Jesus's statements clearly proclaimed that where there is love, there is no divorce, where there is love, there is no retaliation, and so forth. It is clear that all these examples are exemplary and anecdotal. Please note that Jesus does not set these statements up as a legal framework. Jesus is not saying, "thou shall" or "thou shall not." Rather, he offers an example and describes what love should look like in terms of that example.

There are six antitheses clustered in chapter 5 of Matthew's gospel:

1. Anger
2. Adultery

3. Divorce

4. Vows

5. Retaliation

6. Love for enemies

At the end of the antitheses in Matt 5:48, Jesus calls upon his followers to " Be perfect, therefore, as your heavenly Father is perfect."

Imagine that Jesus is looking at a cherry tree. The cherry tree represents a life with all its experiences. Jesus looks at the cherry tree and takes a single cherry, or maybe two. Those cherries are specific situations. Jesus says, "Given these specific situations, what will love look like when it acts?" He is not trying to describe the tree.

If this analogy accurately describes the antitheses within the Sermon on the Mount, the question that needs to be asked is: What holds all of this together? If Jesus is speaking about individual experiences, or cherries, can we look at the sermon and find some of the threads that run through it and bind it together? Perhaps there were two possible threads. First, there is the thread of radicalization. Jesus says there are no oaths where love is. In the ancient world, people frequently swore by God, heaven, or some other sacred entity. Jesus, in effect, says that where there is love, there are no vows. This is radical. Again, Jesus says that where there is love, there is no retaliation—this thread moves the Sermon on the Mount in the direction of radicalization.

The other thread is "interiorization." Jesus's understanding of the law expands it. Now the law not only covers individual acts or behavior, the law also covers people's underlying motives and thoughts. For Jesus, actions and motives are inseparably bound together. The act and the motive cannot be two different things. Jesus understands God's will in this way. Moreover, in God's court, judgment involves both. God judges both the moral motivation and behavior. Giving 10 percent of your income with a poor attitude is less pleasing to God than giving 2 percent with a cheerful attitude. Where there is love, motivation matters, and attitude matters too. The law becomes a spotlight into our interior lives. It is not that acts do not count but rather that acts are bound to their moral motivation. The function of the law is not to simply throw light upon what we do, but also upon why we do what we do.

In God's court, nothing is hidden. All rationalizations are exposed as excuses. Recall that Adam and Eve stood before God naked and vulnerable. The second question God asked was, "Did you eat from the tree?" There is no discussion, there is no rationalization, and there are plenty of excuses. It is clear from that question that everything Adam and Eve say is an excuse. Blaming the snake is an excuse.

The vulnerability we feel under judgment is scary. We often do not fully understand our own motivations. Half the time we are not really sure why we did something. The other half of the time, we are great masters of rationalization. We can always find reasons not to do God's will. Despite our rationalizations, God still asks us, "Did you eat from the tree?"

It seems that with all the interiorization and radicalization that runs throughout the Sermon on the Mount, the sermon could cast a menacing shadow across the face of human existence.

Dealing with the Harshness

If we think of interiorization and radicalization as being harsh or casting a menacing shadow, then we might ask the question: How has the church handled this menace through the centuries? As we might suspect, there have been many interpretations of the Sermon on the Mount. Furthermore, since the antitheses are enfolded within the entire sermon, it is logical to expect that the way we interpret the sermon will also influence the way we interpret the antitheses. Our interpretation of the Sermon on the Mount will throw light upon our understanding of the antitheses. As the church has tried to deal with the Sermon on the Mount over the centuries, it has often sought to moderate Jesus's harshness. The reason for this moderation is that Christians have wanted to implement the Sermon on the Mount into their daily lives. In an effort to do that, the church takes away the rough, sharp edges of

Jesus's harsh statements in an attempt to make his radical words more moderate.

The Beatitudes that opened the Sermon on the Mount have sometimes been a balm to Christians. The opening statements of the Sermon on the Mount note that if we work for peace, we will certainly be blessed. The sermon says "blessed are those who mourn," and who has not mourned loss and death in their life? Certainly, the Beatitudes could help those who have lost loved ones feel better, for the sermon states that those who mourn shall be comforted. Others might see the standards set out by the Sermon on the Mount as beyond what humans can accomplish. They become a goal that we strive for. One way to handle the Sermon on the Mount is to focus on the Beatitudes and edit out the antitheses. The blessings ameliorate or soften the threatening character of the entire Sermon on the Mount. Of course, it is important to remember that the Beatitudes are aimed at those who are outcasts in society. We do not bless the soldiers; we bless the peacemakers. We do not bless those who are comfortably well off; we bless the poor in spirit. If you look at who is blessed, the whole world is turned upside down. Comfort goes to the lost, lonely, and outcast. Jesus wants to make us uncomfortable. Most of us do not hunger and thirst after righteousness, and therefore that blessing could feel threatening to us.

Four Ways

There are four basic ways to approach the Sermon on the Mount. First, the Roman Catholic position has always been that the Sermon on the Mount is addressed to the *perfecti*. By *perfecti* they mean the religious, or those involved in the religious institutions of the church. This could include nuns, monks, or priests. In this interpretation, average Christians are only obligated to keep the Ten Commandments. It is only the exceptional few who are called to comply with the expectations of the Sermon on the Mount. The weakness in this view is that this interpretation results in a two-tiered Christianity: there are lay people and religious people , and one is superior to the other.

Luther and other Reformers maintained that the sermon is addressed to all Christians. All Christians stand within two kingdoms: one foot is in the kingdom of God, and the other foot is in the world. The Ten Commandments function in the world and call us to create justice. The Sermon on the Mount functions within the kingdom of God and calls us to love one another. There are, of course, weaknesses in this position. Some scholars have seen the Sermon on the Mount as a sledgehammer to bash down Christians. They see the Sermon on the Mount as a way to put us on our knees so that God can pick us up in grace. In this view, the Sermon on the Mount has no practical value, but it has theological value.

A third way to interpret the Sermon on the Mount comes from Calvin. Calvin and other Reformers took the Sermon on the Mount and used it as a basis for setting up a political system in Geneva, just as the Puritans would attempt to do in their new home in America. Failure to comply to the Sermon on the Mount often resulted in punishments—for example, the Puritans would put people in stocks. Of course, the weakness here is that the Sermon on the Mount is not a legal document. The Sermon on the Mount cannot be fulfilled by a simple action because it also focuses on motivation. A political system precludes grace.

The Sermon on the Mount serves as a model of a life of faith within a community. This is a fourth way to begin to examine this text. It is addressed first to the Christian community, but in Matt 5:14, Jesus says we are the salt of the earth. It is clear that Jesus expands the idea of community beyond simply the Christian community. Jesus intends for the sermon to be the model for whatever community we may find ourselves in. Jesus intends the Sermon on the Mount to be practiced but always nourished by grace. There is no practice of fulfillment apart from grace. The overarching theme that runs through the whole Sermon on the Mount is love. Particularly love that is expressed in terms of the Golden Rule. Christians know how sin always gets in the way of carrying out the Golden

Rule. Therefore, Christians know that we are constantly driven back to God's grace, but this is not an impediment to practice.

As a model, the Sermon on the Mount excludes vast areas of life. It cannot and does not speak to every aspect of human life. As a paradigm, it offers elements we can apply to other situations. Even though the sermon does not address all aspects of life, these elements do allow us to apply the sermon to other situations. For us, this may mean that the Sermon on the Mount becomes a challenge that forces us to ask: What will love look like here? Of course, there are weaknesses in this position. One obvious weakness is that the Sermon on the Mount says nothing to the systemic, institutional side of life. The sermon is great for talking about personal relationships, but it seems to say nothing about systems and institutions. This leads to one final question: Are individuals responsible for changing the system, or is the system responsible for changing individuals?

About the Authors

DR. CHARLES P. SIGEL received his doctoral degree in classical studies from the University of Pennsylvania. During the 1960s he taught at the Lutheran Theological Seminary in Philadelphia, and during the 1970s he served as pastor of several congregations in Philadelphia. In 1978, he was called to teach Greek and the New Testament at the Lutheran Theological Seminary in Columbia, South Carolina, where he taught for over twenty years. Since his retirement, Charlie Sigel has continued to teach both professional clergy and lay members through his many seminars and classes. He has authored two adult courses: "A New Testament Survey" and "The Parables of Jesus." Dr. Sigel is a member of Good Shepherd Lutheran Church in Columbia, South Carolina.

DR. MITCHELL MACKINEM IS an associate professor of sociology at Claflin University. He is a Sunday school teacher at Good Shepherd Lutheran Church in Columbia, South Carolina, with over twenty years' experience teaching adults and youth. This is Mitch's first Sunday school book, and he has many publications in the field of sociology and criminal justice.